The Gallery of Regrettable Food

The Gallery of Regrettable Food

JAMES LILEKS

Crown Publishers
New York

Published by Crown Publishers, New York, New York.
Member of the Crown Publishing Group.

Random House, Inc. New York, Toronto, London, Sydney, Auckland
www.randomhouse.com

CROWN is a trademark and the Crown colophon is a registered trademark of Random House, Inc.

Printed in Hong Kong

Design by Kay Schuckhart/Blond on Pond

Library of Congress Cataloging-in-Publication Data
Lileks, James.
    The gallery of regrettable food / by James Lileks.
    1. Cookery.   2. Cookery—Humor.   I. Title.
TX714.L555   2001
641.5′02′07—dc21   00-065614

ISBN 0-609-60782-0

10   9   8   7   6

Acknowledgments

Thanks to Institute Patrons for helping build the collection:

George and Nancy Gonzalez; Al Sicherman; Bob Bourgeois; Kristin Blander; Karen Sundell.

If I've forgotten anyone, I owe you dinner. And you choose the recipe.

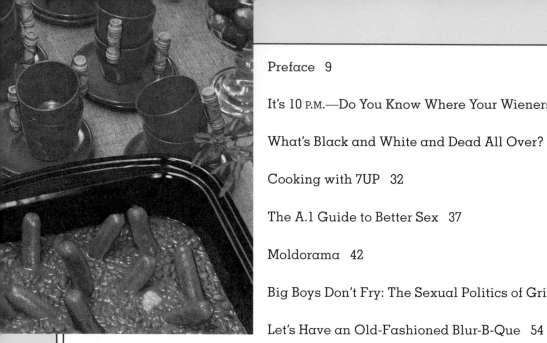

C o n t

e n t s

Preface

On a bright blue summer afternoon in 1962, a woman in a crisp gray suit rapped her knuckles on our blond-wood front door. We'd just moved in to our new house in Fargo, North Dakota, and as local tradition required, one of the neighbor ladies came by with a bag of gifts, pamphlets, ads, and samples. They called it the Welcome Wagon, and one of the sponsors that year was the North Dakota State Durum Wheat Commission. Their recipe book was called *Specialties of the House.* I can just imagine my mom paging through it while the Welcome Wagon lady prattled on about the benefits of North Fargo. Why, there's the Harry Howland Municipal Pool opening next year and, of course, Northport Shopping Center—have you visited the Three Sisters store? It's very smart.

My mother doesn't hear her. She's looking at the books this strange happy woman has brought. And my mother sees . . . this photo.

When the Welcome Wagon lady left, my mother faced a dilemma: she couldn't really burn these recipe books or throw them away; they'd been a gift, after all. Maybe one was some sort of secret manual she'd need some day. Well, she surely wasn't going to cook any of this nonsense . . . so she took *Specialties* and a few of the other books from the Welcome Wagon and put them in the closet. In the back. Under the Rand McNally atlas that no one ever used.

And there these books stayed until 1996, when I discovered *Specialties of the House* in pristine condition. I was astonished. To modern eyes, the pictures in the book are ghastly, florid, gorge-tweaking abominations—the Italian dishes look like what happened when a surgeon gets a sneezing fit during an operation, and the queasy casseroles look like something the dog heaved up on the good rug. Was this book typical of the era? I examined the rest of my mother's collection and began to amass my own, poking through garage-sale residues and rescuing tattered books from dusty bins in antique stores. I discovered that *Specialties* was perhaps the apex of Regrettable Food, but by no means were its dishes unusual in their lurid inedibility. The more I studied the cuisine of these ancient texts, the more it seemed as if the recipes of the postwar era came in two varieties:

1) A cheesy meat dish your family will love!

2) A meaty cheese dish your family will love!

These brochures give a slanted view of their era, of course; if I'd found a recipe book from the American Council on Pork Snout Cookery you'd be convinced that our forebears ate nothing but Snout au Gratin or Cheesy Nostril Salad. But taken together, the books give a unified picture of an era deeply suspicious of flavor.

For example, here's a fictional, but otherwise typical, recipe:

South-of-the-Border Cheesy Meatloaf!

1 lb. hamburger meat

36 lb. flavorless cheese (if substituting spackle, crumble 1 yellow crayon for color)

1 cup dusty crumbs from the toaster

3 grains pepper

1 lb. salt

1 atom chili powder

Mix ingredients, except chili powder, in a turquoise bowl while thinking of Lawrence Welk in a bullfighter's costume. (For extra-spicy version, remember that Welk is naked under his costume.) Put on asbestos gloves; take atom chili powder in tweezers and wave it over meat. Bury chili atom in a lead cask in the basement. Bake. Serves man, wife, and 2.5 children. Enough left over to disappoint family the next night.

I exaggerate only slightly. The introduction to *Specialties of the House* states the case with blunt honesty: "The basic appeal of Durum macaroni foods is their chewy texture and bland flavor." And you could say the same thing about old wet newspapers.

The only spice permitted in excess is fat. Take the recipe for Casserole of Noodles, which is, of course, what you make when you want a break from Noodle Casserole. First ingredient: "two tablespoons of fat." Apparently, back then people had loose, unused fat around the house. The only fat in our house is attached to its occupants. I'm not about to make an incision in my buttock just for a casserole.

Most right-thinking Americans today have a horror of fat, and it's a learned aversion; each gram of fat is regarded as one more bounce on the diving board over an open grave lined with Doritos. Scientists, the priests of the modern age, have sought to banish fat from your life. Take a look at that low-fat cake mix you bought the other day. The powdered eggs and tropical oils are gone. The label now reads: methadrextosepeptidebismolllah 2,4,5, with BHT to preserve freshness, THB to take freshness away, BHT again to say "now quit it!" and put freshness back in, and DDT added because, frankly, they have warehouses of the stuff just sitting around, dragging down the balance sheet.

If these concoctions tasted good, you wouldn't mind. I made a fat-free cake the other day that had a metallic tang; it was like licking a frosted tuning fork. A few years back there was a pseudofat for ice cream called Simplesse, the main ingredient of which appeared to be chalkboard eraser. Ice cream should melt in your mouth. This stuff just decomposed. I think they changed the name and sold it as a shower-tile grout.

Eleanor Roosevelt's favorite

Simply a "hot dog" with mustard on a roll. It's not surprising that the wife of our late president, Franklin D. Roosevelt, should have served this popular American sandwich at their Hyde Park picnic for the King and Queen of England. It's her favorite for *all* her picnics.

And we laugh at the past? At least they had real food with real ingredients. We have NutraSweet, Simplesse, and fat substitutes that require the words "anal leakage" on our snack-food packages, and we laugh at the past?

Well, yes, and we should. If only for images like this:

Why do we point fingers and laugh at the past? Because they just seem so clueless. Their attempts at sophistication look naive and oafish. But there is something else about this 1950 ad from A&P. The copy says:

More "Family Cars" Park Here . . .

It's a pretty good sign, when you see a pram parade lined up outside a store,
that mothers are inside doing a smart bit of shopping.

This image makes no sense at all today. The idea that women would leave their kids outside the grocery store—well, you might as well send out engraved invitations to the local creeps and tot snatchers. But obviously things were different in 1950, or the majority of *Life* subscribers would have been struck by the ludicrousness of this ad.

This curious premise fascinates some modern viewers: might things in the

'50s have been . . . well, better? It's heresy, of course—all intelligent people know that the 1950s were a hideous prison of gray-flannel conformity, a lockstep yes-sir gung ho march to the steppes of Levittown. At least that was the doctrine in the '60s and '70s, when I was growing up. But then something peculiar happened: a revisionist take on revisionist history. After *American Graffiti,* the '50s were suddenly cool. A Golden Age. And now we had a new set of suppositions, equally mistaken. The '50s were not exclusively devoted to the study and pursuit of tail fins, hula hoops, drive-ins, and doo-wop musical combos. They were not "innocent." An era is not preferable to our own just because the cars looked cooler and people seemed to smoke without deleterious health consequences. So what's the verdict? How are we supposed to think of the past, anyway?

The truth of those times won't be found in these pages. These are the commercial bones of the past, what we're left with. They're mostly lies that promise happiness and, of course, they can't deliver it. No sauce, no dish, no spice, no cunning blend of seven secret herbs can change your life forever. Everyone knew that then. We seem to think we're the first people to roll our eyes at the commercial culture; we're not. Even then, no one believed something just because the corporate cookbook said so. But these books don't presume our disbelief—and that's what makes them seem so honest and simple. The quality of the lie is purer; the nature of the fib is cheerful and straightforward.

Did my mom believe that any of these things would make her life perfect? Of course not. I think she kept these books for another reason. Some people smoked, some took pills, some ran to keep off the weight. Mom just looked at the pictures. The recipes kept her slim and lovely for one reason: she never made them.

The Gallery of Regrettable Food

It's 10 P.M.—

Do You Know Where Your Wieners Are?

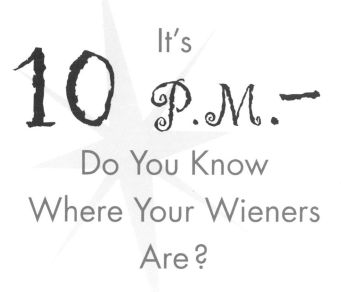

Ah, the life of a cosmopolitan. Late-night guests arriving at the SINFUL hour of 10 P.M., looking for food and drink. Not to worry—you're ready. You're dressed in a white tuxedo. Your wife has been preparing for just such an event by studying her Good Housekeeping *Ten PM Cook Book,* which spells out the precise means for pacifying groups according to their age and gender. In the next few pages, you will be exposed to lurid, suggestive food imagery, so be warned. But that's what you have to expect when you're a night owl—when you're a *10 P.M. cook.*

Especially for the Girls

Hot Perk-Ups

Lemon Float: Heat canned condensed bouillon or chicken broth as label directs; serve in cups; float thin slice of lemon on top of each.

Butter-Cup: Heat canned vegetable-juice cocktail; serve in glasses; float butter pat on top of each with celery stalks for stirrers.

Sherry Cream: To 1 can condensed cream-of-chicken soup, diluted as label directs, add ¼ cup sherry. Heat and serve with a sprinkling of chives.

No, a Hot Perk-Up is *not* what you get when you stuff Mary Tyler Moore into the range. It's what you make for the calorie-conscious Gals: a little hot chicken juice. Or soup with a little booze.

Note the waistlines of these women. Did they keep their intestinal tracts in a hope chest for the day when they might be needed?

If you're wondering what gives these drinks their 10 P.M. specialness, look at the Butter-Cup recipe: "serve in glasses." Ingenious touches like this really impress. And don't forget the celery! Not a minute must pass without a reminder of the need to keep our weight down, thus keeping our mate aroused, thereby preserving our socio-economic status.

"Is this hearts or bridge? I'm too light-headed to tell. Anyway, did you hear about Madge? Seems she stopped sticking her finger down her throat to throw up. Mm-hmm, true. Said it ruined her manicure. Now she uses the handle of a Fuller Brush and she just swears by it."

WHEN IT'S STRICTLY STAG

First of all, the guys want liquor. They want a pistachio cordial that matches their ties, the coffee cups, and the salad and the relish. AVOCADO GREEN, the rutting stags demand.

To remind them that they're men, make sure to embed a batch of wriggling, erect wieners in a sea of beans.

According to the illustration above, it was not unusual in the '50s for a party to include a friend who lacked a body. No one seems to notice, of course; *why, it's 10 P.M.*

19

Remember: if your guests

are as drunk as you are, just shove stuff in a glass and dump sugar on a plate. They're just going to throw it up anyway.

This one goesh to Betty, whosh alwaysh shaying how much she loves fruit. She oughta, she's married t'one. Here y'go, Bets. Bottomsh up.

If you think it's an artful presentation, just remember, it's 10 P.M., and you've had a few.

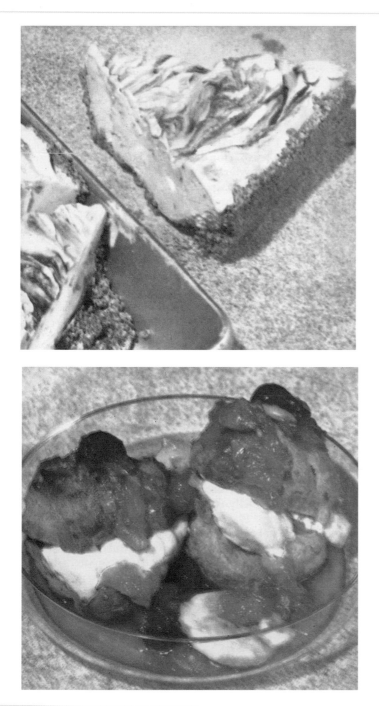

Dessert.

Hey, gang! Who wants a big slice of purply cabbage-cream pie?

 **Perhaps** a nice batch of scones & Pepsodent in a banana-placenta sauce?

Teen-age Triumphs

BENEDICTISH FRANKWICHES

Ah, for the days when "Teen-age Triumphs" meant graduating without a record or a baby.

Proof that sexual frustration—abetted by burger-teasing virgins, cheered on by a better-looking "popular" kid—can turn a kid's hair GRAY.

Unless he's a 52-year-old "friend," who likes hanging around with the teens. He likes their keen spirit; they think he's the creepiest. But he brings liquor.

Frankwiches?

Mom! The gang's coming over for a sock hop in the knotty-pine-paneled basement! Can you make those Benedictish Frankwiches again? You know, the ones that look like creamed tumor balls? Oh, Mom, you're the absolute MOST.

How can you make sure a 10 P.M. party doesn't last past 10:06?

Serve them this.

Somehow, creamed lobster in creamy lobster sauce (with cream) doesn't go well with a bellyful of booze—particularly if the Stags have been hitting the bourbon, and the Gals have been knocking back sherry soup for the last hour. This is a dish whose hue and unrelenting chunkiness prompt a rash of coat gathering, pale faces, and muttered apologies. My, look at the time. Of course, Bob will try this, but Bob's the one who always stays after everyone's gone, and you know what? I don't care if he is the boss's brother, if he heaves in the shrubs one more time he's no longer welcome.

At least not after 10 P.M.

Everyone

gather 'round! It's time for pastel-tinted hairy balls with salsa verde!

Everyone? Hello? Where'd everyone go?

At this point the husband and wife grin and wink: mission accomplished. Empty house, and it's not even midnight.

Honey? Let's leave the dishes for tomorrow. Mr. Frankwich wants to come out and play.

WHAT'S BLACK AND WHITE AND
DEAD
ALL OVER!

The 500 series encompassed many books: 500 salads, 500 desserts, 500 ways to serve thyroids, etc. Daunting, yet thrilling—why, one could make a snack a week and not run out for 10 years! But there are only about 70 recipes per book. By "500," the authors probably meant the number of cumulative portions produced if you cooked everything.

Trust me: you won't.

None of this stuff resembles contemporary definitions of a "snack": when people crave something small and tasty to get them through the afternoon, they generally don't want jellied tongue entrapped in quivering aspic. But this is what they served back then, before the Frito enlightened us all, and premade French onion dip brought savory snacking to the humblest home. Read on, and count your blessings you live today.

You know, most guests really don't like it when the dinner loaf has a spinal column.

This is one of the odd Precambrian dissection projects that pop up in these old books. It appears to be some sort of fossilized carcass covered with cream cheese; the orange wedges indicate the likely location of the limbs. You can imagine this thing scooting around the primordial muck.

Perhaps that circle is not a cross section of a spine, but a blowhole (ahem) of sorts— or a false eye to confuse predators. Put it on the floor and watch it frighten the dog!

What the hell is this? I know, I know—it's a snappy cheese custard snack. But it almost resembles the maw of some carnivorous plant, open wide, waiting for you to tickle the hairs that make it snap shut and sever your finger. (Perhaps that's what they mean by "snappy.")

Do Brazil nuts really add the *nicest* party touch? That's a rather grand claim to make; having staked out the superlative high ground, it suggests that subsequent party

Brazil nuts add the nicest party touch to this snappy custard snack

touches will be nicer, nice, okay, acceptable, and so forth, down to *gawdawful crappiest party touches.*

Yes, it's the *individuality* of the portion that people adore. Most people, when presented some inedible dish that resembles a plate of Horta-fetus calamari, will clap their hands and say: "Whee! It's crusty, it's oozing sneeze juice, and, best of all, I have an INDIVIDUAL portion!"

Nonsense. Your guests will resent you intensely. Individual portions mean the host can tell at a glance whether each guest has finished their portion, left half uneaten, or simply mashed the whole thing up and moved it around to make it look as if they gave it a good crack.

This looks very much like a magnified cluster of warts. Although warts don't usually come with parsley.

Today's assignment: find the chicken.

Your friends
will certainly enjoy
chicken shortcake
when served
individually

Perhaps in the '50s, this was how you broached the subject of a threesome with your dinner guests.

Shape combination aside, these snacks do not look dramatic. Snacks are not required to be dramatic. Once you start to make dramatic snacks, you worry about adding cleverly carved radishes as comic relief. Save the drama for the end of the meal, when everyone's had a second glass of wine and is sitting in stunned embarrassment while the

Snack pastries are dramatic when shapes are combined

Andersons—who've each had three glasses—tear into each other over issues of fidelity and money. That's the stuff of life, the anguish of the human heart; that's dramatic. These are just *crackers,* for Chrissakes.

Cold swollen hot dogs and cucumber slices do not equal "snacks," and they surely don't spell "glamour." In fact, frankfurters are generally agreed to be incapable of assuming glamour unless they are nestled in the cleavage of Grace Kelly. Even then it's arguable.

But at least you see the genius of the 500 series at work: this picture alone probably accounted for 57 of the 500 snacks. Trying to get 500 snacks out of these few pages must have been tough work. Radishes—one snack or two? Well, two, if you don't eat

Frankfurters take on a new glamour in this gleaming aspic

them all at once. . . . Then McCarthy a few desks over threw down his pencil and said, "Ahh, screw it—count the cuke seeds as snacks and let's go get a drink." Another day at the office done.

BALLS ON PICKS

Form these mixtures into balls. Chill. Serve on picks.

ANCHOVY BALLS—Mash 4 ounces anchovy paste with 2 hard-cooked eggs, add 5 drops Worcestershire sauce, few grains cayenne and ¼ cup minced parsley.

CELERY BALLS—1 cup minced celery, 3 ounces cream cheese, ¼ teaspoon salt, dash pepper, few grains cayenne. Roll in chopped parsley.

GREEN BALLS—½ cup grated Swiss cheese, ½ cup minced ham, ½ teaspoon prepared mustard, 1 egg yolk, ¼ teaspoon salt, dash pepper. Roll in minced chives or parsley.

BURNING BUSH—3 ounces cream cheese, ½ teaspoon minced onion. Roll in minced dried beef.

LIVER SAUSAGE BALLS—1 cup liver sausage, ¼ cup minced celery, 2 tablespoons minced green pepper. Rub bowl with garlic, mix ingredients, then roll balls in minced dill pickle.

Perhaps

Balls on Picks is not the best way to get the fellas over for a pregame nosh. The name alone makes men cross their legs. Green Balls and Burning Bush sounds like a married couple sharing a simultaneous STD eruption.

If Balls on Picks don't work, of course, the Aspic Entrées will please the gang to no end. Tongue Mousse seems to refer to those fellows who spit on their hand and slick back their hair.

ASPIC ENTRÉES

TONGUE MOUSSE—Use beef stock and 1½ tablespoons unflavored gelatin; 1 cup mayonnaise; 1 teaspoon dry mustard; ½ teaspoon salt; 2 tablespoons each minced onion, green pepper, and parsley; 2 cups ground tongue.

JELLIED CALF'S LIVER—Use liquid from cooking liver; add 1 onion, minced; 3 sprigs parsley; 2 tablespoons vinegar.

COOKING WITH 7UP

you're
really

COOKING

when
you're cooking
with
SEVEN-UP!

for a new dimension in kitchen cookery
Nothing _does it_ like Seven-Up!

At first, it seems as if they're trying to reassure us. Really! You're actually cooking when you use 7UP! You're not just pouring sugar water into a bowl, you're *really cooking*.

But you're not. You're committing a sin. As you will see over the next few pages, you are joining an odd mind-control experiment conducted by 7UP in the '50s, an attempt to break free from the shadow of the colas and establish 7UP as an indispensable member of the family table. A refreshing beverage. A condiment. A confectionary aid.

"Nothing <u>does it</u> like Seven-Up!" says the cover, and while you can't dispute the assertion, you could say the same thing about caustic lye.

What planet was this picture taken on?

Would anyone have ever decided to try this without the encouragement of 7UP—and even after this nightmare suggestion was offered, did anyone try it? Once, maybe. Perhaps while sick, or drunk. But twice? No.

On the other hand, maybe this is a still from some Jack Webb–produced anti-marijuana film. Imagine his clipped narration: "Betty had been to a marijuana party a week before. Reefer, mary jane, tea, weed, skeezix, grass, wombat smegma, pot—the kids have all kinds of names for it, but it all comes down to the same thing, Mister: it's dope, it's illegal, and it interferes with a woman's natural sense of breakfast."

Finally, one must ask: two bottles? *Two?*

7UP CHEESE-FILLED PANCAKES

2 cups ready-mix for pancakes	2 cups 7UP
2 eggs, beaten	2 tbsp. melted butter

Combine beaten eggs and 7UP. Add to pancake ready-mix all at once and stir lightly. Fold in melted butter. Pour ³/₄ to 1 cup of batter into a greased griddle. Bake slowly until golden brown on underneath side (about 3 minutes). Turn and bake on other side. Place on baking sheet in moderate oven (350°) to keep warm until all the pancakes are baked. Now fill each pancake with a generous amount of creamy cottage cheese, then roll and sprinkle with confectioner's sugar, and top with strawberry preserves.

One
can accept drinking 7UP with one's pancakes: if there's no juice, one could pretend. One can see one's self spearing a piece of pancake with a fork that also contains a hunk of cheese-filled omelette. American cheese, that is. Or Swiss. Any of your familiar nation-state cheeses.

But 7UP pancakes filled with cottage cheese is a combination that makes one put two fingers to one's lips and implore one's gorge: Down, boy. Down.

Baste your Roasts with 7-Up!

One of the most popular kitchen uses for 7-Up is that of a tangy baste for meats and fowl. Seven-Up helps to highlight the natural flavor of the meat.

with BEEF or PORK!

Place your roast in the roaster with lid off until meat is oven-brown. Use only enough water in roaster to prevent sticking. When ready for additional liquid, add 7-Up as required, basting at frequent intervals.

with LAMB!

Start your roast or shoulder of lamb with about ¾ cup of water to create enough steam to last until the meat heats through evenly. Then baste with two or three (7-oz.) bottles of 7-Up, the number depending on the size of the roast.

with TURKEY!

Place turkey in roaster with one cup of water (for steaming). After turkey heats through, baste with three or four (7-oz.) bottles of 7-Up, depending on size of bird.

with WILD DUCK!

You can get the best out of any wild fowl or game by basting it with 7-Up. Seven-Up takes away any "gamey" taste and still preserves the natural flavor.

Here's a capital notion, friends

"Add 7UP as required." Note: when cooking, 7UP is never required.

Dear Duncan Hines: I underestimated the size of the roast and have insufficient 7UP for basting! Will Sprite suffice?

Pass the Coke-soaked yams and the Fresca stuffing, please.

And what have we learned? When dating rock stars, baste them first with 7UP.

35

Just

think: every item shown in this picture was made with 7UP. The ham was basted with 7UP. The wieners, the brats, the stew, the gelatin mold—the UnCola suffuses them all. The partygoers are alight with lemon-lime glee—as a liquor mixer or just a sparkling refreshment. The laughing blonde wears a dress that goes well with the hue of the 7UP bottle. The Nixonian man seated by the fire has a tie that captures the rich deep green of a 7UP bottle.

Take the wiener, Miss. Bite down. Join the tribe. You like it . . . it likes you. It is your *destiny*.

THE A·1 GUIDE TO BETTER SEX

Cooking for a MAN

Tested Recipes to please HIM!

If the way to a man's heart is through his stomach, then this means making an abdominal incision and proceeding upward through the alimentary canal. Not very romantic, really. Better to slap on the A.1 Sauce.

The title of this book reminds one of *How to Care for a Parakeet* and other variety-store pet-care manuals. It implies there's something special about cooking for a MAN, as opposed to any other sort of human being. But the message is clear: it's not how to cook for *a* man, but for the archetypal give-me-meat-or-give-me-death man. And it supposes that such a fellow has never heard of A.1.

Well, at least the recipes are tested to please HIM. A woman might wonder where and when they tested them on her husband, and why he never mentioned it.

Set your Chef's Cap for a Man...

SEASON
with

A·1

SAUCE

**Don't you dress, make-up and hair-do to please a man?
Cook with the same idea in mind; season with A•1 Sauce,
and hear some rave reviews of your home cooking!**

"Don't you dress, make-up and hair-do to please a man? Cook with the same idea in mind." Meaning . . . put garter belts on the lamb shank? Wax the underarms of the turkey wings?

It also helps, apparently, if you wave a spoon half the size of your head. Yes, that's what men want—spoon-waving, face-painted, pug-nosed Lucille Ball impersonators wearing a deflated Mylar balloon.

As for setting your chef's cap for a "Man," it's never been explained exactly how one sets one's hat for a man. No fellow I know is versed in the language of hat positioning. I've never heard a fellow say, "That woman is giving me the eye, and she's hiked up her skirt a little—but her hat's set all wrong. Guess I won't go get her phone number." No one wears hats anymore, so it's less of a problem than it used to be.

It's not certain which caption goes with this dish. The items on the plate actually appear to be Father's kidneys, burnt and breaded. Note the clever instructions for the Oniony Hamburgers: when a recipe tells you to make "6 patties" and later informs you that the yield is, indeed, "6 patties," we're obviously dealing with idiots. Perhaps it's a reference to the bad old pre-A.1 days, when patty mortality claimed one out of every six burgers.

No more! Protect your Oniony Hamburgers with the prophylactic power of A.1.

ONIONY HAMBURGERS

¾ lb. ground beef chuck ½ cup coarse minced
1 teaspoon salt onion
⅛ teaspoon pepper 3 tablespoons A·1 Sauce

Combine ingredients and form into 6 patties. Heat 1 tsp. butter or margarine and 1 tsp. of shortening in skillet until it begins to smoke. Brown hamburgers on each side, reduce heat and continue cooking until done (about 4 minutes). Remove from pan, sprinkle with salt and serve. Makes 6 patties.

FATHER'S BEEF & KIDNEY STEW

How to switch a man from
GROUCHO to GUSTO...

The "before" picture does not suggest a Groucho; he has the expression of a fellow trying to remember whether or not he is Ronald Reagan. Or perhaps the boss snapped at him that day and asked him if his brain was in his ass. Hours later, he's thinking, No, it's right here; why would he suspect it was elsewhere?

The post-A.1 image indicates a steady, constant application of highballs, and bespeaks a level of glee one does not usually associate with steak sauce. Unless it's fermented.

This Man
Hated His Spinach

Somebody has said that men are not divided into bassos and tenors, but into spinach-eaters-and-haters. If you have a "hater" to feed, try a few drops of A · 1 Sauce on his portion of spinach, and see if he doesn't come up for a second helping! That's one challenge A · 1 Sauce has actually met!

G. F. HEUBLEIN & BRO.

HARTFORD, CONN.

Perhaps. More likely, this man has just had his buttocks lanced with a hot railway spike. Spinach evokes passionate reaction, but if the mere presence of spinach made people look like this, Amnesty International would have condemned it years ago.

How, exactly, can men be divided into "spinach-eaters-and-haters"? The hyphens suggest one category: men who both eat and hate spinach. This implies two additional categories: non-eaters-and-haters and eaters-and-likers. (There's also non-eaters-and-likers and non-eaters-and-non-haters, but they are statistically insignificant.)

If Gramps looks like this, it's more likely that the spinach is not to blame, but rather Roosevelt and that damn pack of Reds he has for a guv'mit. Does A.1 soothe the brain of a man inflamed by socialism? The pamphlet is silent on the matter.

These are not salads as the term is currently understood—at least not all of them. *The Better Homes & Gardens Salad Book* contains dozens of tasty ways to serve roughage, and 97 percent of them would be welcome at any contemporary table. Grapes are timeless. Avocados are eternal.

Molds, however, are another matter. One large chapter of this fine volume devotes itself to the quivering solid salad. Of all the items in this book, it may be perhaps the only genre that's truly fallen out of favor.

Is this just a matter of fashion or of style? Perhaps. It's possible that in a few years molds will stage a proud comeback, and citizens of the future will regard the book you're reading now with faint superior snickers. Mold scoffers, what did they know?

If that's the case, we've a limited window of opportunity to humiliate these dishes. Let's get busy.

N**o** need to bother, indeed, as the caption says. This'll finish off appetites one way or another. Dessert? It's a core sample from a mass grave.

Oddly enough, it doesn't seem to have a name. It's Rosy Fruit-cocktail Slices, but slices of what? Why, a Rosy Fruit-cocktail tube. Yes, but a tube of what? Of Rosy Fruit-cocktail Slices. Yes, but slices of—oh, never mind.

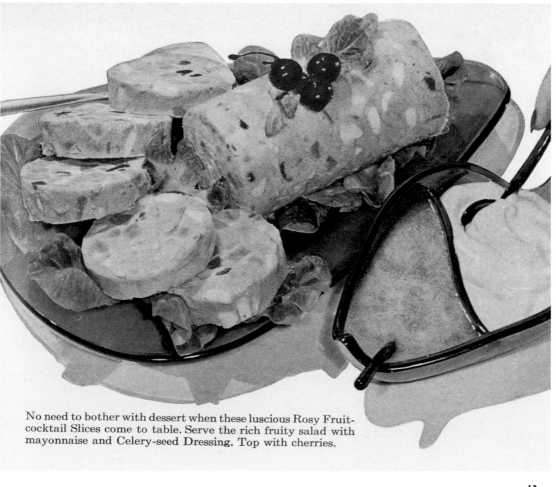

No need to bother with dessert when these luscious Rosy Fruit-cocktail Slices come to table. Serve the rich fruity salad with mayonnaise and Celery-seed Dressing. Top with cherries.

Little Boy,

Fat Man, meet White Guy. Between the Atom Bomb and the Hydrogen Bomb, there was this one: the Gelatin Bomb. It's one of the denser molds in the collection—you could use it as a football if you wished. Imagine the feel of it—like the taut fullness of a pregnant woman's belly.

And it's been polished. One more thing women had to worry about back then: oh, I forgot to polish the molds, and they'll be here any second. . . . Well, a squirt of Lemon Pledge ought to do it. Everyone will just think it's a flavor.

Any guesses as to what this really is?

Snowy Chicken Confetti Salad.

Sunshine Salad.

The copy advises that we give the "traditional pineapple-carrot salad a perk-up trim" by putting a green-pepper flower on top.

The recipe includes vinegar.

In the future, perhaps dense blocks of pineapple-carrot-vinegar mixtures will be considered "traditional," but only if we start making them now. And maybe we should. History repeats itself, first as tragedy, then as farce, and finally as the salad course. Let's just get it over with as soon as possible.

With a quick recipe change, different dress-ups . . .

Another brain mold, this one spattered with indigestible seeds.

You know, when something bears such a close resemblance to a human body part, it would make sense NOT to surround it with red pulpy slices. Watermelon? Sugared muscle tissue? *You make the call.*

I don't know, and I don't want to know. I just don't.

It's a cucumber fun house, perhaps: notice how they seem to be pressing against the sides of the mold, as if demanding our attention. Help! We're being felt up by smelly salmon in here—let us out!

While

everyone was laughing and joking over the roast, the mold evolved at a rate scientists had thought implausible for a salad. With blinding speed it formed a neural net—dendrites snaking from cell to cell, connecting with pimiento nodes, feeding off the olive glands. By 7 P.M. it was self-aware. By 8 P.M. it had developed the

powers of cognition and the ability to observe its surroundings. At 8:32, when it was placed on the dinner table, it realized that it had no mouth and no limbs, and it was completely, utterly screwed.

Big Boys Don't Fry:

THE SEXUAL POLITICS OF GRILLING

A fine cookbook brought to you by Big Boy grills and Kingsford charcoal, this tome reassures men that it's okay to cook. Indeed, according to the cartoon at the front of the book, male-directed incineration of animal flesh has a proud lineage that goes back to the caveman days. Hairy, stinky primates used to stick fly-covered shanks of mastodon over a fire, and no one called them sissies for cooking. Of course, they didn't dress up in elaborate silly costumes and pose self-consciously in front of their womenfolk, who watched with bemused indulgence, but still, the idea's the same: it's MANLY to cook. REALLY.

Big Boy
BARBECUE BOOK
Shows how easy it is to cook on Spit or Grill

$1.00

Answers Most Common Questions
- HOW TO BUILD A FIRE
- HOW MUCH CHARCOAL TO USE
- WHEN IS FOOD COOKING
- WHEN IS FOOD DONE
- HOW TO AVOID FLAME-UP

The full name of this instructive tome is *A Picture Treasury of Barbecuing*, written by Demetria M. Taylor, Home Economics Director of the Tested Recipe Institute. The advantages of BBQing are laid out in the first few pages: "Husbands become the experts and do the barbecuing. Wives take it easy. All they have to do is make the salad and dessert. Become the BBQ Leader in your neighborhood. Your friends will call you the best host in town. Then they'll invite you to their backyards after they've learned your tricks of entertaining in the great out-doors." Be the BBQ leader of your block! Inform on the vegetarians and report them for doubleplus unmeatthink to the Meat Police!

Also, this necessary instruction from Demetria, Goddess of Carcinogens: "Man-sized tough paper napkins are a must for barbecues."

See? It's manly to cook!

So why does the cover of this booklet seethe with desperate attempts to reassert masculinity?

Read on.

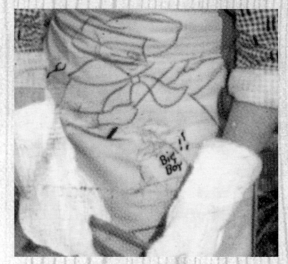

Careful study of the cover illustration shows that the words BIG BOY are overlaid on the groins of both the apron chef and the actual human chef.

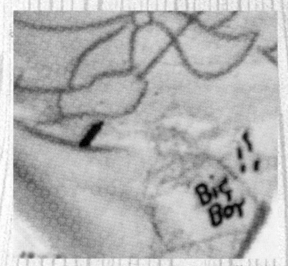

Paging Wilson Brian Key; paging the founder of subliminal advertising theory, Mr. Wilson Brian Key: you're wanted in the Big Boy groin area.

You are still a man if you cook! Particularly if you're cooking meat over fire! *Especially* if you're cooking meat over fire!

Barbecued Party Apples

Core **large baking apples.** Pare a third of the way down from stem end. Place each on a double thickness of heavy duty aluminum foil. Fill centers with a mixture of **sugar** and **cinnamon.** Brush peeled surfaces with **pink-tinted light corn syrup** and put about **1/2 tablespoon butter or margarine** on each. Wrap very securely in foil. Barbecue 1 hour on grill or 25 to 30 minutes on briquets. Apples are done if they feel soft when gently pressed with an asbestos-gloved thumb.

I don't know what this is, but pour enough liquor in a frat boy and he'd have sex with it.

Note the last line in the instructions. Safety first, folks—dispose of the glove the *modern* way: cut it open and beat it on the table until the fibers form a gauzy cloud.

Nothing

like a gooseneck lamp and a bed of coals for making your roast CONFESS!

Gentlemen, this interrogation may confirm our worst-case scenario: we may have a marinade gap.

BIG BOY MANUFACTURING CO., INC. • BURBANK, CALIFORNIA

The
sexual tension has lessened by the time we get to the back cover. The man is older, and either his masculinity is already denuded beyond repair, or his potency is assured by his role as patriarch and Bringer of Meat.

Several interesting elements to note—the spooky dead branches that hang down over the scene, the celestial spirit-sprites in the upper left-hand corner, and the odd garb of the character at the end of the table, who's dressed as if he wants to impress the tablecloth.

Think they have enough gourds?

53

Let's Have an Old-Fashioned

BLUR-B-QUE

The *Better Homes & Gardens Barbecues and Picnics* is an ordinary book, really; publishers turned out these things by the hundreds every year. Each said the same thing—it's fun to barbecue. It's fun to put meat over fire. Use some sauce. End of story. There's really not much more to add.

Or *is* there?

Could this delightful, innocent American pastime have a darker side? Why, yes. Of course. In the background of the pictures of this simple book, we find deeper messages, disturbing tableaus, unsettling images of an America these books never meant to show.

All this plus Pepper Pups! Read on.

Tip

number one: always compare your cooking meat with a small chunk of charcoal. Remove before the meat matches the chunk.

Here, a man demonstrates the procedure. Bill is wearing a matching shirt and oven mitt outfit from Hathaway of Beverly Hills, and his tartan-patterned apron is actually one of his wife's dresses. Donning a dress in public without anyone knowing it, comparing charcoal to chicken while wearing a coordinated oven mitt/shirt ensemble—well, Bill *lives* for days like these.

Suburban innocence defined.

Junior is being served one of Dad's famous Whopper-burgers: they're essentially double-patty burgers with relish and cheese in the middle instead of on top. Wow! We'd *never* have thought of that.

Here's the straight dope on making super-duper Whopper-burgers

Sure, they're great, once you've loaded them with straight dope. But Dad, they're so one-dimensional. Who wants a burger with only one side? Try this new treat:

Two-faced Hamburgers

But there's a dark side in the background. Mom is hoarding the Cokes again, hissing at her daughter: *Stay back! Stay back from Mommy's mixer!*

Everything's just right for a beach barbecue! Except . . . there really doesn't seem to be much to eat

here. There are more packages and carrying cases than actual comestibles. As is typical for this book, the real action is in the background.

1. THE NERVOUS BUSH. Either it's quite windy, or this bush has been watered with crack-pipe juice for the last few weeks. If it is windy, why aren't the paper plates blowing away?

2. THE BUTCHER DISPOSES OF THE EVIDENCE. Upon close examination, it's obvious why no one's

seated around the food. The bright spread was just a ruse to get them to this deserted beach, where they were pitilessly slaughtered by their host. No smoke comes from the grill; it's long gone out. Probably it was never lit: the minute he got the forks out and started stabbing the cantaloupe and stabbing and STABBING—well, homicidal lust overtook him like a cloud of angry gnats. A blowup of the background shows him feeding a bone-colored item covered with muscle to the fire. Probably a thigh.

kets, but it ended up perfectly arrayed! What are the odds? Unduplicatable!

That's one explanation. The other is a little more sinister. More Hitchcockian. In the background we see a woman running toward the car, and there's something about the scene that makes one suspect a crop-dusting plane is right behind her, guns blazing.

This station wagon appears to have thrown up an entire meal. Everything was nicely packed. All the dishes were stowed in the baskets—then the husband mistakenly slammed the gearshift into first and plowed into a fence post; the impact blew everything out of the bas-

Fear, hesitation, quiet cowed submission—the woman tentatively reaches into the basket, while behind her the strange and brutal man she knows only as Marco nibbles a breadstick. It is their way; it is their . . . ritual. Later he will ask her to wear the owl-feather mask, and she will say no. That excites Marco. It angers him, but there is love in his fury, the sort of love she cannot expect anyone to understand.

Spread-out-and-serve basket lunches

Marco is thinking: This is about the stalest breadstick I've ever had.

was spread and the items unpacked. The couple had an amusing argument about why the hell he brought the stupid CARVING BOARD on a picnic, for God's sake—and the crock! You brought the crock of beans? Why do we have all that Tupperware if you're going to drag a CROCK all the way into the country? As they argued, neither saw the boat approach.

It drove up on the grass, and the sailor clambered out with a sheepish grin. He explained he was new at this sailing business. Sorry folks; didn't mean to interrupt. . . . Oh, here's my friend Bob. What were your names? Frank? Jane? Great.

A haunting image, rife with mystery. Where are the people? What became of the happy, hungry picnickers? One can only reconstruct what happened from the visual evidence: the picnic blanket

Do you like to play, Jane? Do you? Does Frank like to play? *Bob does.*

By the time police found this scene, the ice was melted and the beans were cold. CROATOAN was engraved on a nearby tree. No trace of anyone was ever found.

No book would be complete without recipes no one will ever make

Cocktail Totems

Stack 'em high, invest 'em with spiritual properties, pray to 'em, smother 'em in barbecue sauce. They're a snack and a representation of unseen spirit life forces!

Gosh and Golly Relish

No one has ever asked for this by name. No one ever will. People are as likely to ask for Gosh and Golly Relish as they are to request Jeepers and Great Caesar's Ghost Frank Dressing, Land O'Goshen and Lord Almighty Briny Cuke Fragments, and I'll Be Damned and Yer Shittin' Me Semi-Pungent Pickle Chunks.

Pepper Pups

Secret ingredient: pepper.

Hot Chop-Chop

Ah, so! No tickee no eatee!

Shrimpkin

The famous Russian warship staffed entirely by midgets.

Nutty Pups

Secret ingredient: spittle of Jerry Lewis. Also pepper.

Glop in a Pot!

Good Housekeeping's Casserole Book attempts to dress up this messy dish, repositioning the casserole as a gourmet delight, the hallmark of a chef's ingenuity.

No one, of course, believed that for a moment. No one ever imagined Jackie Kennedy in the White House kitchen, telling the chefs she wanted bean-and-lemon-wedge casseroles for the next state dinner. But the average cook might think: if casseroles were all anyone could cook, perhaps these would be Jackie's favorites.

And who can say that they wouldn't have been just that? Read on.

With casseroles, artistry in presentation is less of a concern. People know they're going to get a blurry ragout of flesh and viscous liquid, something that sprawls on the plate like the contents of a liposuction bag.

Beet Pie Casserole.

Da, Comrade Mom!

This is a meal. It is also the scene from *The Andromeda Strain*, when the scientists magnified the image to 300,000X and detected small green extra-terrestrial viral residue in the mesh of a recovered satellite.

Are peas green viral residue? No. Unless they're cooked.

I have no idea what this is. It's the back cover photo, and no recipe in the book seems to take responsibility. It's very bright, though. Lemons seem to be involved, although I should note that I've seen that yellow fluid in another context, and if it persisted beyond two days, the dog went to the vet.

This

is called Monday Pie. The recipe calls for lamb, gravy, and MSG. What an excellent start to the week, eh? Fried strips of albino flesh cunningly blended with parboiled Scottish terrier testicles.

After one bite, husbands probably requested that the wife not make Monday Pie anymore. Just hit him hard on the head with the pot on Sunday night.

FAVORITE
RECIPES
OF
FAMOUS
PEOPLE

LEA & PERRINS
SAUCE

HOW
TO CARVE

Sic Transit Gloria Iturbi

Well, which is it? Recipes or carving instructions? Frankly, were I one of the "famous people," and half of the book was given over to lessons on how to drag a sharp knife through dead flesh, I'd doubt my famousness.

And well they should. While a few of these names may ring some bells today, most earn a shrug and a *huh? Sic transit gloria mundi.* But give them this: if they made a cookbook today, they wouldn't include classical musicians. You'd have Whack MC's Bitch Sauce or Spleefy M'Blunt's Chronic Stew.

At least nowadays they'd have the decency to animate this horrible eyeless bottle. It has no sight . . . it has limbs . . . it has no brain . . . it must CARVE, and CARVE some more.

But what is it carving? Delights await.

This

does not look like a leg of lamb from the Stork Club. This looks like a breast of stork from the Lamb Club.

And who the hell was Sherman? The founder of the famous Stork Club, of course. So he has the right to claim this as a Stork Club favorite. But you'd think he would have chosen a more visually appealing dish than this. Supper ought not to resemble a skinned cat. Unless, of course, that's what you ordered.

Sherman Billingsley's
LEG OF LAMB—STORK CLUB

Jose Iturbi's
SPANISH STEAK

Make that *sic transit gloria Iturbi.*

This is some of the most tortured, attenuated garnish a steak has ever had; it looks as if El Greco had attempted to paint the mask from the *Scream* movies.

It's unclear why you'd need lessons on how to carve this thing. All you need to know is where to stab it in case it leaps from the plate and goes for your throat.

But who *was* Jose, anyway? Why, a Spanish concert pianist, of course, known for his Mozart. Quick: know any contemporary Mozart interpreters who'd be well known enough to be used in a popular steak-sauce brochure today? Of course not.

Beware

of meals whose names consist of a city and a genre. Salmon loaf doesn't tell you much, but you have reasonable expectations of salmon. Ditto meat loaf; one assumes it contains meat. So London Loaf contains . . . what? Thames sludge poured into a Bundt cake ring, perhaps. ("Grease pan with lampblack; strain sludge through the undershirt of a Cockney bricklayer.")

Lowell Thomas'

LONDON LOAF

I don't care if Mary Margaret McBride was a pioneering broadcaster; this is just plain *foul*. Burned wieners in a drunken scrum, jostling and molesting what appears to be a rectangular, exsanguinated brain.

Mary Margaret McBride's

LINK LOAF

Ellery Queen's
POTTED VEAL WITH DUMPLINGS

Potted:
not a word that gets them running to the table nowadays. Plants are potted. Drunks are potted. Food ought not to be potted. No man ever tosses down a menu and tells the waiter: *Whatever you got that's potted, I'll take it, pal.*

Note: Since Ellery Queen was not a person, just a pen name for a consortium, perhaps this is actually a photo of the brain trust that wrote the books. Eight pulsing brains. *Potted* brains.

HORRORS

from the Briny Deep

USES and PREPARATION *of* MAINE Sardines
America's all-round Seafood

MAINE SARDINE TOMATO SURPRISE PAGE 11

Fish makers face a challenge when presenting their foods to the public. While fish may be tasty, healthful, and offer something more subtle than the rude charms of beef, it looks like pale, flaky pink clay, or it seems to promise little more than a scaly glistening mouthful of coagulated mercury.

The following images are taken from the days before jets and vast, fast distribution networks. Midwesterners in the '50s never saw fresh salmon. "Fresh" meant the can at the market didn't have half an inch of dust on its top. A variety of books provide these images: the salmon people do their best to reshape the fish into other forms, while the sardines people say to hell with it—these are dead decapitated fish, and there's just no sense pretending.

Says the caption: "Salmon Cocktail—a delicious way to start a dinner."

1. Isn't salmon . . . pink?
2. Could this possibly be bloody cauliflower *masquerading* as salmon?

Furry

treats. These are nut-slathered salmon rolls, but they bear an unfortunate resemblance to severed shanks of sheep shins.

Hostess Rule #7: finger food should not look like breaded fingers.

The canned salmon industry's biggest problem: your cat wants this more than you do. As Bob Dole would put it, You know it, your cat knows it, the American people know it.

Never mind. You can always distract your guests with some blood-drizzled eggs and lemon wedges. It's simple! Everyone's doing it! Just cut yourself on the jagged edge of the can as you try to dislodge all the salmon, then shake your finger over the canapés while hopping, swearing, and trying to remember when you last had a tetanus shot.

The sardine industry has a similar problem: no matter what they do, their product looks like fish torsos with the tails and heads chewed off. Which, of course, is exactly what they are.

If you'd like to disguise this fact, just smother the piscine torsos in a vinyl sauce colored

 with melted peach crayons.

Note: If you let this dish stand for an hour before serving, it will not move even if you turn the plate upside down.

DRECK

from Foreign Shores

When I was growing up in Fargo, we had two foreign restaurants. One served Italian. The other served "Chinese" food, such as chow mein. (You could tell you were in a foreign restaurant when rice was served as a side dish—alone, in a bowl, not buried under a glop of casserole.) Most Fargoans seemed content with this arrangement. But I'm sure there were those who'd been to far-off lands—Minneapolis or Milwaukee—who'd sampled the rich array of foreign foods; surely there were frustrated housewives who curled up in a chair in the middle of the afternoon with a cigarette and a cup of coffee, reading of exotic menus in a magazine, dreaming of a place where they didn't have hotdish every Thursday night, a place where the smart set met to talk about cultural things over interesting meals. . . . Then the pickup pulls into the driveway. . . . She hears the clatter of his engine: *macaroni macaroni macaroni.*

Let us now jet off to foreign lands to see what delights they offered the palate in 1964.

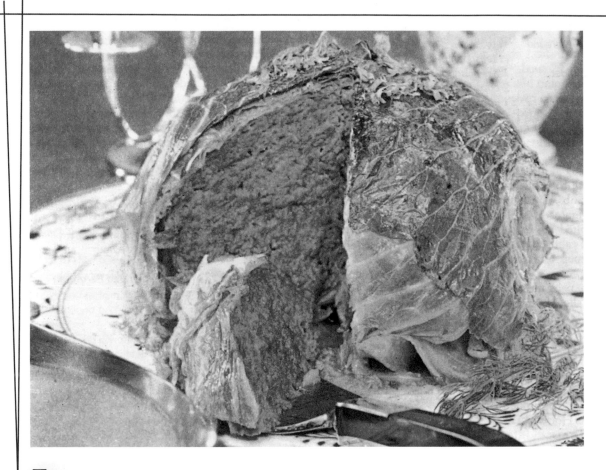

It looks like a cross section of the Swamp Thing's brain, but it's actually cabbage stuffed with hamburger. Stuffed? It's engorged.

This would seem to defeat the purpose of serving a leafy vegetable.

Nonetheless, meat lovers will worship it: Finally! That's how you do cabbage! Bravo! It's a Trojan Horse infiltrating the encampment of militant vegetarianism.

Origin: Danish. Main exotic ingredient: about 36 cups of horseradish. Likelihood of American acceptance today: zero.

This

illustration for the German section represents the peak of Hun cuisine. Foreign food at the time often meant plates like these: brown from stem to stern, shiny with the juices of beasts, best washed down with gallons of beer.

The overall inedible nature of the food can be discerned in the tableau on the beer stein: the gentleman seems to be giving his food to a dog under the table.

Ach, du lieber
HDL, HDL, HDL.
Ach, du lieber
sauerkraut,
sodden mit fat.

down Mexico way

After a Mexican meal—break a Pinata!
Make a gay papier-mache parrot (*below*);
cut a small hole in back; fill with favors,
and hang from ceiling. Blindfold guests and
let them bat away—for fun and surprises!

This sounds more like the makings of a private sex party for Tory officials, frankly.

Sausage Smothered in Red Cabbage

Serve the sausage chopped for those who enjoy a leisurely meal. Or serve it uncut for guests who prefer to grab the meat, run to a corner, and bolt it down while growling at everyone else.

Sausage Smothered in Red Cabbage? I think they have the title for this one backwards. It would seem to be the other way around: Red Cabbage Smothered in Sausage.

And now, as at the end of an old variety show, when all the acts gather on the stage to sing a farewell song, we have the players from every nation blaring out a discordant salute to dyspepsia. You don't know where *not* to start.

Note the shrimp (top center), arranged to resemble a Caucasian tarantula extricating itself from a glass. We also have our old friends the egg and olive penguins, whose appearance always makes people smile and say, "Look—penguins made from eggs and olives." No one ever eats them, because we all know they're held together with toothpicks, and there's some- thing about the unexpected spearing of one's hard palate that spoils a night of gustatory exploration. Even if that *is* how they do things in foreign lands.

This book covers dishes from HOT to LAN, an odd designation that gives the book an encyclopedic air it doesn't really deserve. What dish starts with LAN? Twice-baked LANolin-moistened towelettes? LANced toad boils? What starts with LAP that couldn't be included in this slender volume?

It's an utterly ordinary book for its time—meaning, it contains some unbelievably regrettable dishes. But let's imagine that every cookbook in Western Civilization was lost, and only one survived. What if that single tome was the HOT-LAN Volume of the Family Circle Illustrated Library of Cooking: could they reconstruct our culture from this sole example?

Let's see.

Illustrated Library of

Family Circle COOKING

VOLUME 10 Hot-Lan

HOTDOG HAPPENINGS:
Dozens of Ways to Use This
All-American Favorite

**INFALLIBLE INSTANTS
AND MIXES**
Shopping Tips and Tricks

**THE JOY OF COOKING
FOR OTHERS:**
Gifts to Make or Bake, Pretty
Party Foods for Every Purpose

**LAND OF PLENTY
PRESERVED:**
Processing and Canning Tips
and Recipes for Jams, Jellies,
Preserves and Pickles

What would future generations think about this scene? The frankfurters' picnic! It's another hot dog scrum, and it all seems so innocent and carefree: rustic athletic franks photographed in boisterous play. But then you realize that they're all tied together, pushing on one another. It seems to me like the ones at the far right are doubled over in agony—the ones at the left are leaning back.

Then, a few pages later, we see . . . this. It's supposedly a mold of some sort, but when you put it in context with the picture above, you have to wonder if this isn't some hot dog version of the freeze-dry process used to deliver Han Solo to Jabba the Hutt. That's why they're struggling: they know what's coming.

Judging

from the proportions suggested by this fork, this dish is about three inches wide—which makes it a triumph of miniaturization. It's the latest craze: Bonsai Fondue!

The ringed food appears to be a dense, compacted mass of grubworms and lawnmower bag clippings; in the center, it's Rhinovirus Ragout with sliced canned mushrooms. Garnish with batter-fried smelt heads. Serve in a room whose lurid color and off-kilter angles suggest the lair of a villain on the *Batman* TV show.

Salmon Salad Tart

The scholars of the future would decide we had made great strides in food science. Why, just look at the food math: *premade mix* crust + *canned* salmon + *process* American cheese + stuffed olives = dinner.

Ordinary people would want fresh salmon + real fresh good cheese + stuffed olives, but obviously that would result in an inferior product. Why else would the holy HOT–LAN book demand we eschew the fresh and the natural? Didn't chemicals make their lives better? All bow down to the American Process!

And so the future ends up just like our past.

It's the 1950's
and Everyone's Human but Mom!

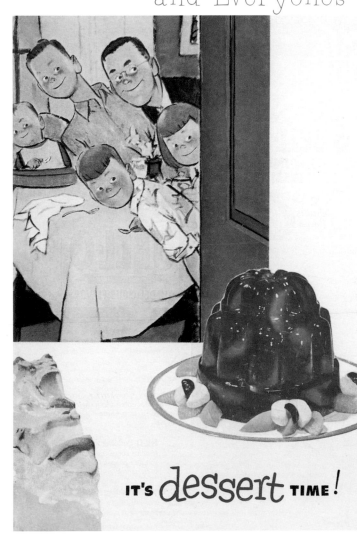

IT'S dessert TIME!

Oh, it surely is dessert time. The whole family strains to get a peek at what's in store. They have to get a peek, because Jell-O has no scent, and therefore cannot be detected by their olfactory apparatuses. What will it be? Surely Mom had time to whip up something between all four well-spaced pregnancies. Perhaps she won't come out for a while—and when Dad goes to investigate, he finds her bent over the sink, weeping.

They all look like YOU, she sobs.

Father does his best to console her, because, well, it's true, it's a blessing that the kids look like him. It's not that he doesn't love his wife. It's just that . . . well . . .

It's just that Mom is a HIDEOUS MALFORMED GORGON.

Her bony arms, her clawlike feet, those mouselike ears—sure, she's sweet and loving, but she's drawn completely differently than the rest of the family.

These Fruits Sink **

Apricots, canned
Royal Anne cherries, canned
Peaches or pears, canned
Pineapple, canned
Raspberries, canned
Fresh orange sections
Fresh grapes
Prunes or plums, cooked

These Fruits Float

Apple cubes
Banana slices
Fresh grapefruit sections
Fresh peach or pear slices
Fresh raspberries
Fresh strawberry halves
Marshmallows
Broken nut meats

And she just gets so enthusiastic about the strangest things. Making the kids memorize these peculiar distinctions—who cares? Okay, you're on a boat and it gets a leak—grab some apple cubes. But is it necessary to cheerlead over this?

Then when she finally settles down and makes Jell-O, it's always something *weird*. It's so embarrassing to have your friends come over and get *this;* you could just *die*.

Jell-O ignores the

GELATIN DESSERT

Joys of Jell-O

Stare at this photo long enough and it really starts to bother you. It's just . . . wrong. It's what happens when you feed LSD to Iowans, perhaps. This is as surreal a juxtaposition as their minds can create.

The "Joys of Jell-O" no doubt capitalizes on *The Joy of Sex;* in someone's basement there's probably a copy of *Everything You Wanted to Know About Jell-O (But Were Afraid to Ask),* or *The Sensuous Chef,* or any number of books that combined Age of Aquarius hedonism with humble, quivering desserts.

There's more. So much more.

difficult '60s!

As with most diseases of this variety, early detection is the key.

Here, an MRI scan shows that the nodes of oversaturated cherry Jell-O have spread throughout the delicious, refreshing prune-flavored foam. Prognosis: dessert!

Perhaps there are situations where you are happy to be served this for supper. Perhaps there's a time when you clasp your hands to your breastbone in genuine surprise and say, "You actually have radishes in cherry Jell-O already made—and in two distinct shapes, as well?" Perhaps.

CHERRY WALDORF SALAD

At first I thought this was a crown of some sort—perhaps for the ruler of a very stupid and equally pink nation. Then it looked like a cap you'd wear to blend in if the locals all suffered from significant head boils. But I realize now that it's a basket of food.

This cunning mold allows people to eat the shapes of various foods without having to taste the actual flavor of the items.

WE COME FROM FRANCE TO CONSUME MASS QUANTITIES.

Hail this trio of quivery Coneheads, three of the loudest desserts Jell-O has ever created. The item in the foreground continues the '60s theme of radish-based molds; the item at the right appears to contain chunks of entombed cauliflower; the mold in the back contains cukes and tomatoes.

How do you cut one of these things? Where do you start?

Ah, finally: slabs of tomatoes, green-pepper flecks, cukes, and olive-flavored Jell-O in an individual portion. But don't stop there: use that wasted empty center as a staging ground for more Jell-O—a second story of Jell-O—*a whole new level of Jell-O!*

As lurid and excitable as '60s Jell-O was, you'll note it existed in a vacant landscape devoid of humans. No cartoon people, no servants, no elegant swells going about their moneyed ways, occasionally interacting with Jell-O.

All that is about to change.

Jell-O: The Groovy '70s!

Urgh.

To anyone who grew up in the early '70s, this picture might trigger a wave of revulsion: it brings back a period when it seemed as if puffy pseudo-Peter-Max-style graphics were used for everything. They announced bad children's movies; you can imagine this artist doing the credits for *Captain Frabdapulous and his Crandigulous Autogyro!* or some other piece from the Sid and Marty Kroft crap factory. These graphics were used in commercials, in educational programming, on toys, in comic book ads. Why? Because the adults of the time kindly wanted their young ones to experience all the hallucinatory effects of drug use, without the long-term side effects. As you'll soon see.

Just

think: this kid with the Mikey coif is now old enough to start worrying about his prostate.

But he had no worries then! Not with Jell-O. And remember, kids, Jell-O is the next best thing to drugs. Or vice versa. Something like that. But it's clearly hip and mod and cool and fab and bitchin' and groovy and all those other adult words the 10th-grade kids use.

Jell-O Gelatin is a *young* dessert. Cool and sparkling. Fresh and fruity. And the colors are pure pop art. (Next time you pour boiling water on the powdered gelatin, just watch those colors come alive.)

Yes, Jell-O is a bona fide participant in the youth culture, in the nationwide enshrinement of randy, sensation-craving, dope-addled monkeys as the arbiters of what matters. The colors ARE coming alive! Wow! And my hand's leaving trails when I wave it in the air!

What flavor was this again? Oh, right: *red* flavor.

Here,

the nuclear family enjoys a nice Jell-O dessert. Dad's thinking about how cool he looks: hey, honey, look at this, it was the widest collar they sold, *and I got the last one.* Notice how small a role the actual dessert is playing. Remember the gigantic torso-sized Jello-O molds at the beginning of this chapter? Now, as befits the grim America of the '70s, expectations have been lowered. Gas will soon run out. Inflation will consume our savings. The children will work for soul-crushing, Rollerball-sponsoring multinational corporations. In this world, *be grateful you have any Jell-O at all.*

Almost 58 percent of American women looked like this in 1974.

What's

different about this image? What sets it apart from every other picture in this collection?

Right! Which makes you wonder about the four tall glasses of Jell-O parfait at the right. Some sort of integrationist's dessert, perhaps? Probably not, which means that if the hostess of this party was white, she may have looked at the dessert and had a complete bolt of panic: *Ohmigod, they're going to think I made a black dessert because they're black!*

The picture violates one of the main rules of photography: never make the pregnant woman in the striped muumuu look as if she is emerging from the custard bowl.

As for the other guests, well, this woman appears to have stepped out of a Breck ad, and this fellow is modeling the popular Gomez Addams look, which was all the rage in the '70s.

Ding dong!

From the age of tuxedos and servants to the egalitarian age of . . . this. Leisure suits, broad speckled ties, lapels like the wings of a 747, straight-part hair, corn-fed Brut-soaked beefy golf dolts with their Hillary wives.

A few years after this picture was taken, a London punk Mohawked his hair and put a safety pin through his clothing. These people, and all they represent, are the reasons why. They're Johnny Rotten's parents—and I thank them for it.

Submit to the Power of Ketchup

Behold:

Wilma and her love apple Godman. The unusual being to the left was the Heinz spokescreature in the '40s and '50s—a tomato head with human features and a monocle covering a horrible, dead, empty eye. Why? Had he suffered the same blinding fate as Mr. Peanut? No: earlier ads show Mr. Tomato Head in Southern garb—string tie, aristocratic plantation-owner clothing. Think Colonel Sanders. He was a symbol of the fine breeding of Heinz tomatoes, and in those days, a monocle meant sophistication. He faced the same dangers as other anthro-pomorphic figures: why, if the Heinz company ever ran short of good tomatoes, they could smash his head open and extract the seeds nestled in his pulpy viscera. But he probably didn't worry about that much. Spokescreatures never did.

He has a rather fey stance here—the classic curve of ancient Greek statuary. The woman is holding an oversized bottle of ketchup, and her smile says Yes! YES! Introduce me to the myriad wonders of ketchup-based cooking!

She was. Now it's your turn.

**Fluffy Omelet
with Crimson Sauce**

Mmm-mmm!

Deep-Fried Frisbee in Crimson Sauce. And what, you ask, is Crimson Sauce? It's . . . ketchup. With onions. But when you think about it, that's a perfect name for plain old ketchup. Sure beats Corpuscle Gravy, anyway.

Satan himself could not invent so fiendish a dish: Deviled Onions!

Get out the fire extinguisher! Slather the tongue with asbestos! Lay in a supply of unguents and skin grafts! This recipe is inhumanly deviled, full of the fires of hell itself—as the last line in the recipe proves. Beware!

37 DEVILED ONIONS

4 large or 8 small onions
⅓ cup Heinz Tomato Ketchup
⅓ cup water
1 tablespoon butter or margarine, mel
¼ teaspoon salt
Few grains pepper

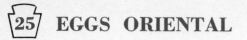

25 EGGS ORIENTAL

1 cup sliced fresh mushrooms
⅓ cup chopped green pepper
¼ cup butter or margarine
1 can (10½ ounces) Heinz Condensed
   Cream of Mushroom Soup, undiluted
⅓ cup Heinz Tomato Ketchup
2 tablespoons milk
½ cup grated process American cheese
½ teaspoon Heinz Worcestershire Sauce
½ teaspoon salt
4 hard-cooked eggs, sliced

Sauté mushrooms and pepper in butter until tender. Add soup and remaining ingredients except eggs. Heat, stirring, until cheese melts; add eggs. Serve over hot chow mein noodles or rice. Makes 4-5 servings.

Ah, so! Velly solly to be humble coolie-egg for honorable housewife. Please accept apology for being slanty-eye cackleberry. Please to be pouring Britisher sauce and Yankee cheeses on undeserving eggs to reinforce and underline historical correctness of Opium War and support for Taiwan. Confucius say: When making Eggs Oriental, it necessary to break eggs.

Hah! Hah! Beloved religious figure humbly submits to role in Amelican jokes. Chop-Chop!

11 BARBECUED CHICKEN

2½ to 3 pound fryer, cut up
¼ cup shortening
Salt and pepper
1 tablespoon Heinz Vinegar
2 tablespoons Heinz
   Worcestershire Sauce
1 tablespoon Heinz 57 Sauce
¼ cup Heinz Tomato Ketchup
1 tablespoon sugar
Dash tabasco sauce

Heat oven to 350°F. (moderate). Sauté chicken in shortening until brown on all sides. Season with salt and pepper. Remove to baking pan. Combine vinegar and remaining ingredients; pour over chicken. Bake 50-60 minutes or until tender, basting frequently with sauce in pan. Makes 4 servings.

Well, it's another Quisling. Another Dahmer. Just another chicken who's just *toooo* happy to be cooking up a fragment of his fellow bird that was ripped from its body, severed by a high-speed industrial saw, and tossed in a fecal stew before being shipped off to house-wives everywhere.

Better you than me, pal!

Note: It's uncertain whether this dish contains *enough* Heinz products.

FOR FAMILY-PLEASIN' VEGETABLE DISHES
cook with _Ketchup_

If vegetables are the problem plate at your home, try some of these flavorful suggestions from the Heinz Home Economics Department.

33 HARLEQUIN SPINACH

½ cup chopped onion
2 tablespoons butter or margarine
⅔ cup Heinz Tomato Ketchup
1 tablespoon lemon juice
½ teaspoon chili powder
2 pounds fresh or 2 packages frozen
   spinach, cooked, drained
¼ cup grated process American cheese

You know, I think "vegetables" are the least important of the many "problem plates" in this household. Mr. Rotarian down the block has a secret life, apparently.

What's missing in this meal? That's right: meat. It's got everything but actual substantive food. The ratios are all wrong—all the ingredients look fine until you hit that deal-killing TWO POUNDS of cooked spinach.

If this guy actually walked down the street in 1954, they'd have beaten him to death.

It's

a Peckinpah porterhouse! We start with the finest cut of beef, then attach several exploding bags of fake blood. Garnish with eggs; detonate; let congeal.

For extra smiles around the supper table, remember the secret to *gooood* cooking with ketchup: *always leave a glistening inner tube of fat on the meat.*

And in case your family's aggregate cholesterol level hasn't spiked into the lethal zone yet, add eggs. LOTS of eggs.

FOR TRULY DISTINCTIVE DESSERTS
cook with <u>Ketchup</u>

Well, there's no disputing that statement, is there?

Here's the example they give: Ketchup–Pistachio Cake.

And for truly distinctive dinners, cook with ketchup, tinfoil, and small ground-up Lego fragments! Good? Nay—but *distinctive.*

FAMOUS CHEFS FORCED TO USE

MARSHMALLOWS

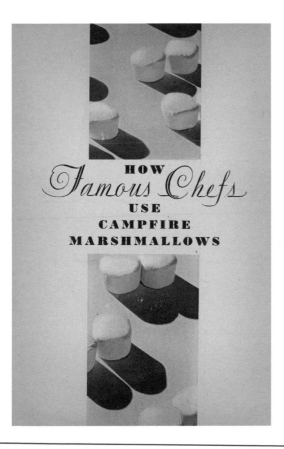

I'll tell you how: with a heavy heart. With a scowl on their face. With the depressing certainty that their professional reputation will plummet to the cellar if anyone ever sees this ghastly cookbook.

This was a project from the Campfire Marshmallow Company, an attempt to make marshmallows a delicacy. By printing the marshmallow recipes of famous chefs, people might regard these puffy delights as a sign of breeding and taste.

Whether the chefs thought this was possible was another matter.

The project was hampered by one small detail: when attempting to convince someone your product isn't just for campfires, it would help to remove "Campfire" from its name.

Prepare to meet our happy, happy chefs.

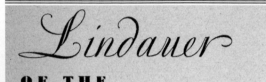

Lindauer

OF THE "ILE DE FRANCE"

Lindauer

—whose first name is undoubtedly Karl— appears to be posing for his war-crimes wanted poster.

His bio says he was also a chef in Algiers, Fez, and Tunis; he was obviously head of the Reich's covert DessertCorps, a much-feared outfit that practiced a new form of mechanized cuisine: with their frightening "blitz-cake" techniques, they could provide dessert for thousands in a matter of moments.

His contribution is a cake with 13 half-marshmallows on top. This would leave one extra half-marshmallow behind. Such a thing no doubt bothered Lindauer greatly. If there was one thing he despised in desserts, it was *imprecision*.

Roemer

OF THE PALACE HOTEL, SAN FRANCISCO

Roemer

seems lost in a private reverie of doubt and regret. Perhaps he is the only one of the chefs who actually took the assignment seriously, only to discover he could no more cook with marshmallows than any of his colleagues. But whereas they were content to take the money and turn out Marshmallow Scorn à la Flambé, he had tried. Really: he tried. He had experimented all night, all day,

into the next night, 'til dawn touched the spires of San Francisco . . . but all he could come up with was this.

Pathetic. A pie with marshmallows on top. It shrieks of failure; it says: Roemer has lost his touch.

He will give the money to charity. He does not deserve to spend it on himself.

Charles

says, Come on, hurry up. Take ze fargin' picture already. Ah am beezy. Too beezy for this crep. Zo beezy I should keek you right outta ma keetchen, but no, Ah will stand here looking dashing in my very dashing way zat makes ze ladies queever. For them, I make deeshes like you will never see. For you, I make the Marshmallow Soufflé. Take a soufflé. Put marshmallows around it. *Voilà.* Now go away—I have lost my pencil and must find it.

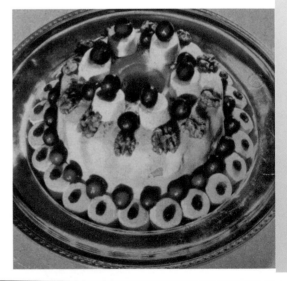

Sabatini

THE NEW DELMONICO'S

Sabatini is the merriest soul in the book, the only chef without airs or pretensions. Perhaps it's because he's been kicked up to the management level—he's sitting by the phone, writing an invoice, not exactly slaving over a hot pot of polenta.

On the other hand, he managed to dash off *two* imaginative meals—peppers baked and stuffed

with a creamy marshmallow sauce, and apples baked and stuffed with a creamy marshmallow sauce.

Perhaps *everything* at the new Delmonico's is served with a creamy marshmallow sauce.

Kircher
OF THE RAQUET CLUB, PHILADELPHIA

Kircher

contemplates his work. He has created the Campfire Marshmallow Fairy, a work of stunning simplicity and paradigm-breaking ingenuity. A lesser man would have put whipped cream on top of the marshmallows. But the Kircher touch, the Kircher element of sheer genius requires that we subvert the old ways! We put the marshmallows and nuts on top of the whipped cream!

Genius! Take that, you old men of the Academy, with your outmoded ways of thinking about nuts!

OF THE BELLEVUE-STRATFORD

Kurtz
may get the award for the chef who put the absolute minimum amount of effort into his creation. From the kitchens of Kurtz, we have something he calls the Virgin Islands.

It's marshmallows over ice cream.

Mr. Kurtz, one suspects, had more important things to do the day they called up and said the recipe was three weeks overdue.

Amiet

OF THE PALMER HOUSE

Amiet looks like a decent soul. He wouldn't be out of place in a Dutch Renaissance painting—as the earthy burgher, or perhaps the honest tradesman at the tavern.

Here is his contribution: marshmallows liquefied on toast.

He brings it to you himself; it's the Palmer House tradition for the chef to deliver the dessert. As you eat it, you study his homely face . . . and you begin to see hidden cruelties in those eyes, those loveless lips, in the flare of the nostrils.

You like? he says, abruptly.

You nod: yes, yes. Actually, it was rather cloying, but . . .

He turns and leaves.

You think: did I see that face in the post office the other day? In a picture? On the wall?

Better Homes & Gardens
MEAT COOK BOOK

Over 400 meat recipes
How to buy, store, prepare and serve

MEAT!

MEAT!

MEAT!

Mmmmmeat!

I love the stuff, myself; it gives me everything I want in a meaty meal: salt, flesh, salty salt, salty flesh, and that great charred taste you only get from the flame-blasted body of an ignorant dead ruminant. That's what meat eating is all about. No vegetarian can dissuade me: when it comes to the disgusting truth of a meat eater's diet, I'm way ahead of them.

And now, thanks to the pictures to come, you will be, too. Let's be like Mr. Geek Chef here—unroll your sleeves, button your cuffs, fasten your salmon-colored shirt up to your chin, and get ready for MEAT. Because meat is ready for you.

SUN

This

would seem to be a segment of an intestine from some creature that ingested the fender from an old DeSoto.

It's brilliantly aerodynamic, this meat. Very modern, nicely streamlined. It's the sort of meat that would perform well in a wind tunnel. It echoes the architectural themes of the 1939 World's Fair; if they'd had a Meat Pavilion, it would have looked like this.

Note! The vegetables are strictly ornamental. Feel free to leave them untouched. These are boiled banquet carrots, grown to accompany meat dishes at social functions. No one eats them. No one ever eats them. Every night, all over America, 48 tons of cooked carrots are thrown away.

Serves the bastards right for their impudent proximity to MEAT!

This is not meat. This is something they scraped out of the air filter from the engines of the *Exxon Valdez*.

Were I to hazard a guess, I'd say the recipe book has it wrong. They call this a roast, but it's actually an angel food cake *topped* with steak. A big hit at the Elks Lodge socials.

Note: The vegetables are strictly ornamental. Do NOT eat the vegetables. Parsley will make you vote for handgun registration. It's been proven SCIENTIFICALLY.

It's

steak à la Ugarte! When decorating your meat, make sure to arrange the onions in the shape of Peter Lorre's face.

Garnish with small, inedible onions. WARNING! The carrots here are not to be eaten. Your manly meat-a-rifficness will diminish if you eat the carrots.

Onions, however, are acceptable. We call onions "nature's steak lackeys."

One

of the more popular cuts: pressed shank braised with smoker's phlegm. It may take a few tries to get Uncle Hank to hack up enough Lucky Sauce, so be patient.

WARNING! Eating the carrots or the parsley will cause your testicles to retreat into your body cavity. Don't even *chance* it. Eat the MEAT.

This has a name like Snowplow-Cut Butt Steak, or something. It's one of those attractive meat meals that brings out the muscle striations to nice effect. You *really* want to know you're eating muscle when you tuck into a plate of meat. Muscle: ask for it by name!

Note how they think that shredding the greens and sprinkling them on potatoes will make us eat vegetables. Hah! Nice try! We'll scrape 'em off and throw away the knife. How's THAT?

I'm really not feeling well anymore.

This is a hocks 'n' brats concoction; it resembles some hooves stuffed and boiled until they explode. Note, to the right, the small figurine of some ruminant, facing away from the meal, blessing it with an offering of methane and hay gas.

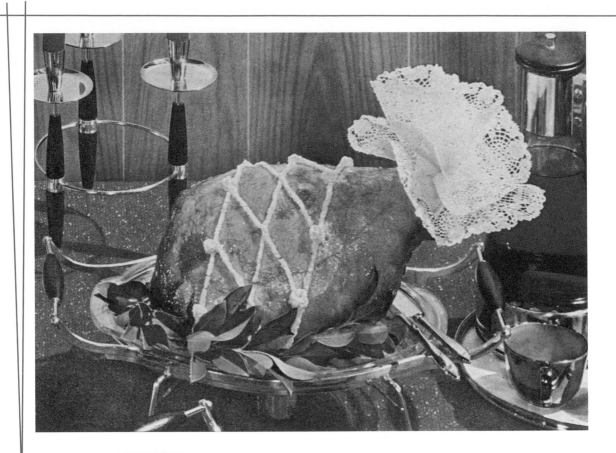

Sometimes

meat likes to dress up and feel pretty. That doesn't mean *anything*. Lots of men like to wear nice frilly things, soft things, just for the way they feel. Some very masculine men are cross-dressers; is it any surprise that the manliest of foodstuffs should sometimes feel the same way?

Mr. Peanut, Chef of Chefs

This booklet was designed to incorporate legumes and legume-derived essences into standard everyday cooking. Like others of its genre, it suffers from excess glee, monomania, and a relentless desire to insinuate the product in question into every aspect of the daily meal. On the other hand, it includes instructions for making penguin statues out of boiled eggs, and for that it deserves special commendation.

Unfortunately, it hails from the era when the cartoonist's craft had been demolished by a preference for hastily drawn sketches; anyone expecting the urbane, 3-D Mr. Peanut will be disappointed. In the '50s things looked "modern" if they were sketched by art school hacks who drank three martinis for lunch—hence the amateurish fellow above. Will Mr. Peanut return in all his full-shelled glory? Read on.

Never

really thought of him this way, eh? Chef of Chefs! He seems less suave and cosmopolitan when dressed in cookery garb, but perhaps now we know what happened to his eye: he lost it when hot oil spattered on his retina.

He wants you to do many things:

Try Taste Thrills in Deep frying

Thrills? Only if you have to get things out of the oil using your fingers.

The illustration seems to suggest that you might enjoy frying up some charcoal briquettes next time you're in the mood for a snack.

Show New Skills in Shallow frying

Try taste thrills! Show new skills! Peanut MC be bustin' mad rhymes!

Shallow frying doesn't seem to have caught on like deep-frying. As for medium frying—well, don't ask.

Here

two Mr. Peanuts appear to be gazing with pride and wonder at several breaded and deep-fried Hershey's Kisses, each covered with spiced ejaculate.

But what this scene really needs . . . is a penguin.

You've already seen the penguins earlier in the book—they were a ubiquitous garnish in the 1950s. It may never have occurred to you that hard-boiled eggs, olives, and toothpicks can create unconvincing penguins, but here's the proof once again. These penguins are captaining a fish-shaped boat bearing a cargo of aspic gelatin and parsley. Ahoy!

250 WAYS
to prepare
POULTRY *and* GAME BIRDS

Poultry for the Glum

Talk about dark meat. This is one of the more regrettable entries in the famous 250 Ways series—it's full of moody, black-and-white pictures of dead chicken. The result looks like a cross between a WPA project to hire unemployed photographers and a menu catering to misers. Nothing here looks good.

What's more, some of these pictures are so tiny that you can't tell what the meal is supposed to look like. But there are two cases where you can clearly see the full horror, and once again, you have to ask: *what were they thinking?*

Cinch up your gorge, and proceed.

Isn't this cheerful? Dig right in to a nice pot of congealed bird chunks. Special bacteria-laden wooden utensils provided for your convenience.

This
is a chicken loaf of some sort, but it looks like a dissection project from the Cambrian era.

Sunday supper will be gayer
for this chicken fruit salad

Why do I doubt this?

You will enjoy spaghetti
more than ever as à la diable

Provided

you don't mind the stink of brim-
stone when you pull it from the
oven.

Believe

it or not, this is an enlarged picture of that delightful dish: Roasted Pigeons.

The pigeons appear to have curled together to comfort one another in death.

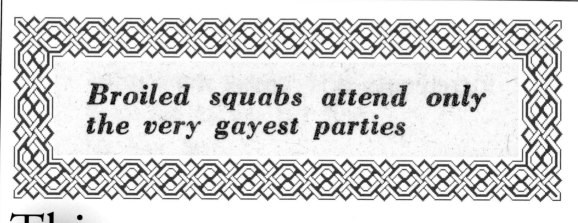

Broiled squabs attend only the very gayest parties

This photograph also is enlarged. It's the ever-popular Jumble of Strewn Squabs.

And it might just be an uneducated guess on my part—I know nothing of the habits of squabs—but I don't believe that broiled squabs have the volitional capability to discern whether a party's gay enough for them.

They're *dead*. They go where they're taken.

Ahh, Mr. Jones! Chilled Monkey Brains!

So you're going to serve a ...SALAD

So you're going to serve a salad! So you're going to try the most basic element of the dinnertime table! So you're a newlywed who hasn't a clue! So you're actually consulting a pamphlet to learn how to make a goddamn salad! So you're still wondering if married life is supposed to be like this, what with the endless boredom during the day, the bleak expanse of a Levittown yard out the kitchen window, the bitter wives down the street who meet for coffee in the morning but don't invite you over! So your husband already seems tired and distracted when he comes home late! So you think a salad is just the trick! So you're right where we want you! So you'll do what we say and buy what we sell!

So let's get started!

With the olive oil a Spendthrift be;
With the vinegar a Miser, of course;
For seasoning needed a Wise Man true;
And for stirring it well — a Madman will do!

This seems to be a rather complex mnemonic device to employ for such a simple dish, and it's more baffling than enlightening. Okay, be a spendthrift with the olive oil; that's clear. Glug it over the greens until the fronds form a small atoll in a sea of liquefied Vitalis: yum. Be a miser with the vinegar, and why? Because the company isn't selling vinegar, that's why. They sell olive oil. Use as little vinegar as possible, lady; those bastards over at Heinz don't need one more nickel than they already got.

But here's the line that confounds: "for seasoning needed a Wise Man true." It makes no sense. Perhaps they mean "the act of seasoning truly required the judgment of a wise man"—but even if that's the case, there's no correlation between wisdom and a knowledge of apt spice application. Go down to the Supreme Court dining room. Watch them eat. I'll bet good money that David Souter puts pepper on everything.

A cheerful note from the days when mental illness was ha-ha-ha-FUNNY: the madness of the spoon is indicated by Napoleon's hat, since it's a well-known fact that madmen regularly regard themselves to be Napoleon. But since European history isn't taught in schools anymore, what will the insane spoons of the future claim to be?

Veal Ring Salad

This resembles the ultrasound prospective parents don't want to see.

Or . . . it's human finger bones jammed into a cat brain, wrapped in a nice bow, sealed in aspic. At least you can give this to the madman who stirred the salad.

The very name makes one blanch; if poor calves are going to suffer the hideous misery required to make them into veal, they deserve better than this.

Say ahoy to Barnacled Scrod! What this is doing in a salad book, I've no idea. It has french fries, some sort of fillet soaking in a light black sauce, and three strange nodules fastened on the fillet like nautical parasites.

It seems to be the antithesis of salad, unless you count that dispirited heap of humiliated greenery in the corner, and I don't.

Kids

will love the new Vermin Salad—a cute and informative way to teach them about common pests and their relationship to city-clearing plagues.

Maybe this is a rabbit—the carrot would suggest so, but it doesn't look fluffy and have floppy ears. Nor does it look like it would hop. If it is a rabbit, it would make consumption a bit uncomfortable. First you use the fork to sever its head . . . then you gouge out a haunch . . . now the torso . . . blurgh! That's enough. Ah, here comes the main course. . . .

$It's$ hard to figure out what this is. Deviled lymphatic tissue and overboiled parsley, perhaps. But it's nestled in a shell of iceberg lettuce—so it must be a salad!

So you wanted to make a salad, eh? Are you satisfied now? ARE YOU? Oh, stop your weeping. It *sickens* us.

Land sakes, that's tasty Lard!
AUNT JENNY
explains it all

Dear, dear Aunt Jenny. For years she put a happy face—indeed, a very happy face—on the proletarian cooking glop known as Spry.

If ever there was a woman born to be shown in black and white, it was Aunt Jenny: with her sensible gray outfits, gray hair, gray-scale skin, and gray store-bought dentures, her grayness only set off the pure dazzling whiteness of Spry.

And what was Spry? Vegetable shortening. Triple whipped for creaminess, too—let those double-whipped bastards over at Crisco beat that. (They did, eventually; Spry isn't made anymore.) But it wasn't just a cooking ingredient—Spry was the means by which men were placated, tamed, and domesticated. It was the balm that troubled young wives stirred into their neophyte biscuits. It was the substance that allowed one man to lord his wife's french fries over another's. It was a can of clouds handed down to the pantry of mortals. If Spry was fire, Aunt Jenny was our Prometheus.

It also made you sterile in large doses. That's just a guess. But Jenny doesn't have any children. And yet she bakes . . . and bakes . . . and bakes, cake after cake, platoons of cookies. Every night she probably threw three pies, two cakes, and 93 cookies out the back door for the birds and the bums. And then she went to bed planning the next day's cooking. Old Can-a-Day Jenny, they probably called her at the market.

To the left is Calvin—you'll meet more of him later. But you'll meet much more of Jenny. More, perhaps, than you needed to see.

Hey, Jenny—Don't fergit yer hubby Calvin!

CALVIN'S CORNER

HOW DID YOU EVER DECIDE WHAT RECIPES TO PUT IN THIS BOOK OF YOURS, JENNY? WHY, YOU MUST KNOW THOUSANDS!

WELL, CALVIN, I KNEW FOLKS WOULD WANT RECEIPTS FOR EVERY DAY—NOT TOO FUSSY OR HARD ON THE POCKETBOOK, BUT GOOD-TASTIN'. THESE SURE ARE—AN' SO DIGESTIBLE EVEN A CHILD CAN EAT 'EM, FOR THEY'RE ALL MADE THE Spry WAY

Calvin's happy, as well

he should be; Jenny's happy, too. And why not? Plucked from rural obscurity to national fame—just the ticket for shooing Old Man Depression out the door. Note Jenny's use of the word *receipts* for recipes—this local colloquialism gives her more credibility, makes her Just Folks.

Aunt Jenny notes one of Spry's most famous attributes: it's *digestible*. This would seem an odd thing to note about a cooking substance; it's almost like saying "an' a body can eat it all up without gettin' the grips, or throwin' it up in a black stinkin' mess on the tiles, too." But she has a powerful pride for Spry's digestibility; you can imagine that she repeats the word while cooking. It's a good baking mantra—round, pliable, the sort of word your tongue loves to knead. Digestible. Digestible. Digestible.

So happy are Jenny and Calvin that they don't note a rather disturbing feature: the cover of her book features the two of them in the exact same pose, discussing the book.

How is this possible? Are they playing out some little marital

game? Perhaps the book was printed weeks ago. Months ago. Last year. But when Jenny's feeling a little, well, down, Calvin says, "I reckon you need a little bout of cover posing, Jen." She picks up a pie, he puts on the special cover suit—worn only on these occasions now—and they pretend to revisit the moment when the recipe book—the *receipt* book—first arrived.

I'm so durned PROUD of her! An' Spry money means I don't have to work!

CALVIN'S CORNER

Here's Calvin gloatin' over one of my tasty strawberry shortcakes. My, but he IS so fond of 'em! I make the old-fashioned biscuit kind and the tender Spry crust just melts in your mouth . . . try it!

If we didn't know Aunt Jenny and Calvin, we'd suspect she poisoned him and posed him just *so,* ever remaining in the grateful posture of Spry-induced delight. Calvin doesn't seem to be looking at the shortcake. Calvin doesn't seem to be looking at *anything.* Perhaps Calvin has been full of straw and formaldehyde since he complained about the biscuits one too many times. Norman Bates, meet your dream girl.

But that's not our Jenny, not our Calvin; he loves her and she loves him. Still, it seems like a lot of shortcake for two people. Perhaps old Cal has a wooden leg, or one of those flinty farmer metabolisms that lets him shovel back the shortcake by the bushel and never gain a lick of weight. Then again: euphoria and sugar cravings often indicate heroin addiction. Care to roll up those sleeves, Uncle Cal? No; I thought not.

Moments like this make us forget we haven't had sex in 30 years!

CALVIN'S CORNER

144

CALVIN ALWAYS LIKES TO LICK THE SPOON IF HE'S AROUND WHEN I'M MAKIN' FROSTIN'! HUSBANDS AREN'T MUCH DIFFERENT FROM LITTLE BOYS, ARE THEY, LADIES?

No, they surely aren't . . . messy, silly, foolish creatures. Handy, I suppose, but just little boys you can lead around by their pee-pees. Why . . . all you got to do is . . . well, lick the spoon handle from time to time, and they'll do almost anything for you. But doesn't that just make you mad, ladies? DOESN'T IT? I declare, sometimes it makes me so mad I could just spit.

But I can't spit in the Spry; that'd be wrong.

Still, ladies, we all know how humiliating it can be when the mister comes back from town stinkin' of rye and ceegar smoke, and he wants a little of what he calls "comfort" or asks us to do our "duty." That's why I mix a little saltpeter into every cake.

When I'm makin' frosting, I use my special receipt to make sure Calvin isn't makin' frosting later that night. If you know what I mean.

Oh, we have our ways, ladies; we do have our ways.

Nah, I ain't much different from little boys—why, lately I'm wettin' the bed again!

CALVIN'S CORNER

Speech bubbles in image: "OH, AUNT JENNY, I'M SO FED UP ON ALL THOSE JOKES ABOUT BRIDE'S BISCUITS" / "AN' THERE'S NOT A WORD OF TRUTH IN 'EM. NOW, ANYONE CAN MAKE GOOD BISCUITS. JUST FOLLOW THIS SPRY RECEIPT CAREFULLY AN' YOU'LL SEE!"

One

month into the marriage, and she already wants OUT. She thought it would be different—how, she can't say: oh, it's not as if Bob isn't sweet; he's just . . . changed. He seems to think she should always be there waiting at suppertime with a goddamn basket of biscuits. Is that what's ahead? Forty years of getting snapped at because she's made another batch of "bride's biscuits"?

Why, she never cooked a thing before she got married, and now she's supposed to turn out 10 tons of fresh bread a day? Help, Aunt Jenny. Help.

Aunt Jenny smiles, passes along the magic word—Spry—and pours another cup of her whiskey-laced coffee.

That's one of her *favorite* receipts.

Aunt Jenny seems radiantly young here, as though she draws her life force from the misery of the biscuit novice.

I had my eye to the keyhole every minnit she was in the livin' room!

CALVIN'S CORNER

One of the more poignant images in the Spry books. Some neighbor's kid's wandered over to "Aunt" Jenny's kitchen for some of her treats. Jenny's the "Aunt" to all the kids; you can just hear her say "Now, you just call me Auntie," as she hands them a Spry-laden cookie, and watches their smiles as they gobble down the goodness. It's apparent from these books that Jenny has no children of her own; either her womb bore no fruit of its own accord, or Calvin was shooting blanks.

Not that Cal seems to be the sort of fellow worried about that sort of thing.

Elmer—a uniquely odd name for a child in any era—caws about his mom's inadequacies; Jenny cheerfully offers to lend her expertise. Oh, it'd be temptin' to poor-mouth Elmer's momma, make him depend upon Jenny for cookies—but it wouldn't be right. Besides, they have their own problems. Elmer's momma has to work because her husband's off on "an extended business trip." That's what she says. No one believes it, but you got to give the woman the right to some dignity.

Of course, given that little Elmer appears to be drawn into this picture, or inserted by means of some rudimentary photomontage, it's possible he is meant to symbolize Aunt Jenny's hallucination. Perhaps the kids never come around. Perhaps all those days of telling new brides how to cook with Spry paid off, and they're all bakin' up a storm for their Elmers and Elmerettes.

Well, good for Spry! That's what matters, when you get right down to it.

CALVIN'S CORNER

Sometimes Jenny dreams 'bout children an' wakes up cryin'!

AUNT JENNY STARTS A BRIDE OFF RIGHT

little Spry fixes all, as we see from this charming little comic strip concerning eight days of a failing marriage. Or does it? In the third panel, the husband seems a little too enthusiastic, as though he is mocking the entire nature of marital happiness. And by the fourth panel he has the same fixed stare and frozen mask of rapture that we saw earlier on Calvin. He's entered . . . the Spry Zone.

Back to the first panel: it's odd that the new bride considers a giveaway shortening cookbook a grand gift, let alone one appropriate for a wedding present. But why is she worried about her cooking? All she had to do was look at the back of the booklet.

The Adoration, or Aunt Jenny Instructs the Domestic Angel. This cover is so loaded with high Renaissance iconography I don't know where to start. Jenny is pointing to the can of Spry, just as minor saints in devotional paintings draw our attention to the Baby Jesus or some other figure whose veneration was required. The Domestic Angel—whose hair seems spun from a nimbus of golden light—clasps her hands in the posture of worship. You see this gesture in many Italian Renaissance paintings; also in many '50s ads for washing machines and milder dish soaps.

The artist has made the Domestic Angel's gaze appear to float between Jenny and the Spry, as if she is simultaneously overwhelmed by gratitude to Jenny the Baptist and in awe of the power of Spry.

They are shown against a crimson background, symbolizing the blood that is shed if you're not careful with the jagged edge of a metal can.

CALVIN'S CORNER

Why ain't I in the pictures no more? Mebbe I'm DEAD!

Here's Ebenezer Todd and Hank Parsons about to lay into one of my meat pies. Poor men don't get any good home cookin' at the diner down by the depot.

Let us all pause and bow our heads in respect for a time when the first sentence of the caption above was considered a *single* entendre. This statement seems to contradict everything we know about diners—aren't they the lonely man's source for good, stick-ter-yer-ribs nutrition?

You get the feeling Ebenezer never misses any church suppers. You can be certain Jenny doesn't—it's an occasion for a redoubled flurry of Spry deployment. No one even bothers to make pastries, biscuits, cakes, or pies for the suppers—why bother? Jenny just comes in with all of her stuff and puts it right in the middle of the table. Oh, it's not like she pushes other stuff out of the way. Not exactly. It's just unusual how Mary Johnson's meat pies end up at the edge of the table, so folks got to lean over to get 'em.

DURN it! The minnit I head off t' my reward, she's lovin' up the local hoboes!

CALVIN'S CORNER

Here's our postman, Fred Cooper, samplin' some of my cookies. He says I make the best ones in town. But say, it's no trick at all to make nice crisp, tender cookies with Spry. You just try it!

Well, it's just plain nice to get a fella's attention, that's all. Nothin' wrong with that. Calvin's been gone a decent time now. It's not like she's taking a ride with another man, or sitting next to him at church. She just asked the postman in for a cookie before they got all stale. And if tongues want to wag about that, let 'em wag. Lands sake, Fred's practically 80. They don't even give him much mail anymore—they let him do his route with a bag full of circulars, and let that new fella Egon handle the important mail. Half the time they find Fred in a bush somewhere asleep with his drawers all messed up. Poor man. Is it so bad to bring him in and give him a smile? Make him feel like a lady enjoys his company? If that's sinnin', then you can have your church and your Sunday socials. Let's see who brings the meat pie next time.

What was it, 30 years ago? Forty? Fred was the smartest lookin' man in town. Big as a sturdy oak, handsome as all outdoors, good with a horse; he cut a fine figure. All the girls loved him, 'specially us silly schoolgirls who'd watch him pass and then get all giggly. 'Course, he was older 'n us. But then there was that unpleasantness with my friend Marthy . . . no one talked much about what happened, but Fred left promptly after that. Joined the Rough Riders—folks say he was there with TR when they charged that hill. He

came back home, tended his folks' farm; never did marry. Got called up in the Great War on account of his previous service. They say he took some gas that made him simple. I don't know 'bout that. But he was different when he came back. Almost like the life had just plain gone outta him. Spent a lot of time down at the GAR hall with all those old men, talkin' about wars.

How he got a fed'ral job in front of all the other able-bodied men 'round the county, no one knew; might have just been an act of pity. No one really begrudges him that. Folks remember what he was and they don't blame him for what he became. The Lord loves us all. If a body can't give him a smile and a cookie from time to time, well, it's hard to say what bein' a Christian's all about then.

He does smell, though. You got to open the windows and pull back the curtains when Fred pays a call.

Oh dear God in heaven . . .

CALVIN'S CORNER

152

It's safe to say this woman hasn't shaped a cutlet with her fingers in 40 years. That's something the servants do. Marthy and Aunt Jenny grew up together. Marthy was the daughter of the town banker or perhaps the farmer who had the biggest acreage in the county. She always had everything growing up—best carriage, best horse, best clothes— she was the most popular girl in class. Beautiful singing voice, too—Lands sake, it was like listening to angels. All the girls wanted to hate Marthy . . . but they just couldn't.

It was hard sometimes to watch from a distance; see Marthy grow up, leave town for that trip to New York—imagine!—and harder still when she married the Wilson boy. Between her inheritance and his family money, well, no one knows why they still stay 'round these parts. Guess it's nice that they do: on a Sunday afternoon, it's a pleasure to watch their friends from the city come up in their motor cars—they all must have one fellow whose job it is just to shine the bumpers. At night when the air's clear you can hear their parties; a body can just lay in bed with the windows open and hear the laughter and the music, and imagine being there with all those pretty people.

Well, what do they know 'bout Spry? Nothing.

Still, it's always good to see Marthy. She was one of the first to come 'round after Calvin passed on. It's nice that she takes an int'rest in my Spry receipts. And it's nice that she invited me to come with her into the city. We both know I never will go, though. She has her world and I have mine.

There are times when Marthy gets all upset over the littlest things— a run in her silk stockings (she's got 50 pair if she's got one) or something her dog threw up. There are times I just want to say to her: "Marthy, chill your mixture!" And sometimes I say just that.

CALVIN'S CORNER

Jenny, it's COLD an' I cain't SEE an' I'm all ALONE.

153

AUNT JENNY SHOWS BRIDE SECRET OF CAKE SUCCESS

AUNT JENNY, JACK'S BOSS IS COMING TO DINNER. GEE, I WISH I COULD MAKE CAKES LIKE YOU DO!

DON'T FRET! YOU CAN MAKE A BEAUTY THE NEW SPRY WAY AND IT'S SO EASY, TOO!

SPRY WITH **CAKE-IMPROVER** AND THE ONE-BOWL METHOD

Well, it's a living, pushing Spry, but it does make a body tired sometimes to hear these ninnies worry about their cakes. To tell the truth, there are days I don't need it—no sir. Calvin left me a goodly sum; I have the money now to dress up. Why not hire someone else to be Jenny for a while? There's that woman who sends me pitchers, says she looks like me . . .No, folks'd catch on.

At some point Aunt Jenny's got to wonder: when are these silly bitches going to learn to think for themselves? When are they going to stop soaking their dress shields every time the boss comes over for supper? Go to the bakery! Buy a goddamn cake! Anyway, you think Jack'll get fired because his wife's cake wasn't up to snuff? Liquor the boss up during the appetizers. Come DEEsert time he won't notice and he will not care.

Sigh. Why not enjoy life? When will it be *Jenny's* turn?

Boo!

It's good to know Jenny made it into the age of color newspaper ads. This one hailed from a Sunday supplement in the late '50s.

After this . . . nothing. A decision was made at Lever Brothers HQ—they needed to update their image, modernize the line. The whole Aunt Jenny thing was just too much Grand Ole Opry for contemporary tastes. Sure, it worked once—

We'll meet again, my dear sweet Jenny . . . oh God! I miss you so!

CALVIN'S CORNER

when there were millions of newly minted housewives desperate to learn how to fry food. But that was then.

Did they send someone to break the news to Jenny? Did they just write a letter, or make a phone call? What did she think when she heard her services were no longer needed?

Forgotten in an instant. Cast aside, her stories lost in a flash. Until now.

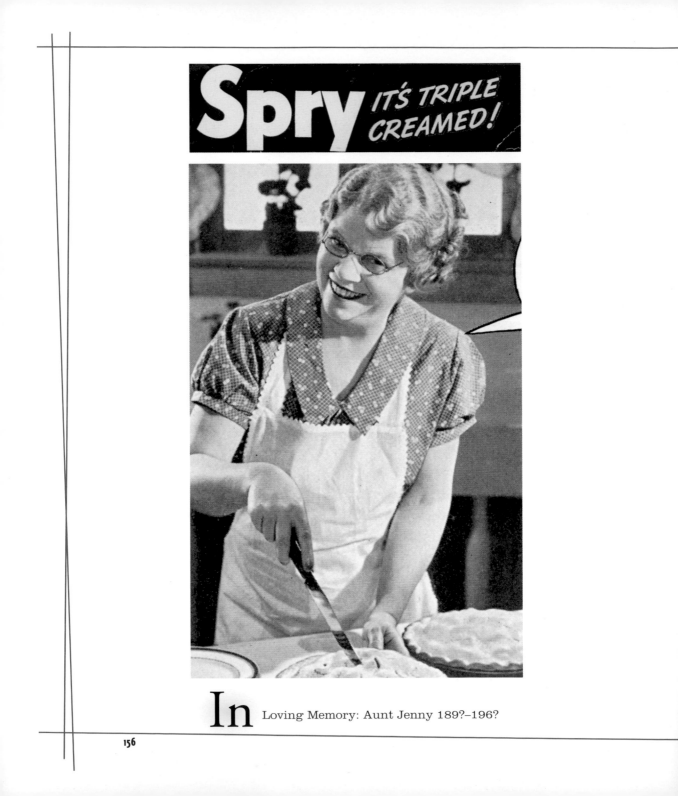

In Loving Memory: Aunt Jenny 189?–196?

When you think of chicken - think of Swanson!

Swanson's *Parade of Lost Identity*

In the '50s, Swanson solicited recipes from the women of America, and repaid the winners with disembodiment. Their heads were ripped from their bodies, their names shrouded in the thick cloth coat of their married names. Most of the women in this cookbook have no first name of their own, no last name—only the dull thudding syllables of their husband's name, preceded with the horse collar of MRS. Not all are lost to history; as you'll see, one of these women was rescued from obscurity. But for every one who was rescued, dozens were lost. Draw near, gaze upon their floating faces, and pay heed to the lost women of Swanson's.

Mrs. August W. Beikirch

All hail Mrs. August! This stolid matron gave her name and body to bring us this mold. We don't know if she had a name such as Greta, or Elaine, or perhaps Monica, or if her last name was something euphonious and melodic. All of that was lost when she was joined to August Beikirch.

Swanson's repaid her for her sacrifice by making and photographing her favorite dish: Lanceable Boils with Fat Sauce.

Mrs. Ernest A. Stockburger

Another
victim of the Meaty Name of Marriage—whatever tender sound she may have answered to before her wedding day, she was Mrs. Ernest after that. And her new last name—well, you can practically smell the fat and seared cow flesh.

Her dish is fairly ordinary and utilitarian. Potato chips are a garnish, a ruffle, and an edible part of this delicious chicken whatever-it-is. You get the idea, however, that Mr. Stockburger was not a man of means. Perhaps they ate a lot of beets and potato chips in the

Stockburger house. Perhaps she wore that big black hat a few more years than she would have liked. Perhaps everything went wrong because everything always went wrong—that's just how it is with some people. But perhaps she kept her good spirits and kindly ways intact all through the years and never complained. Perhaps getting a spot in this cookbook was the best thing that ever happened to her, and certainly the most exciting.

Mrs. Leavenworth Wheeler

Hair

by Jiffy Pop. This poor woman was cursed with a name one can only hope was no reflection on her marriage. What did she call her husband? Levvie? One can only hope she didn't name her son Quentin.

Oddly enough, her chicken dish seems based on the 19th-century prison-construction theory called the Panopticon: prisoners are housed in a circular building with all cells observable from all vantage points. Either that or she had one too many nightmares of giving proctological exams to Martians.

Mrs. Myrtle O'Dell

Hey ho the merry oh! Cheery as she seems, there's a touch of the Kamp Kommandant to that steely smile: ve have vays of making you eat chicken.

Myrtle's contribution is one of the least appetizing of the batch—one of those puke-in-a-bowl-and-shove-it-in-the-icebox surprise dishes that occur with alarming frequency in the Gallery. Garnish with shaved things; serve with whipped lard.

Mrs. Usher F. Newlin

Again, a nice young woman cursed by her husband's curious name. No one gives newborns names like this anymore.

She has the strange glazed look found in early advertising illustrations—say, for Wistoria Croup Balm, or Palmer's Curative Elixir. Her meal is a chickeny version of meat loaf, with a decorative addition so pathetic it's rather touching; no doubt it came from another booklet called *Decorating with Olives!* It's a push-button chicken loaf! How modern.

Mrs. Richard S. Atwood

Hubba! Again, a high school picture, perhaps taken from a group shot with "The Gals," everyone beaming happily at the future. The meal is disturbing, though—chicken meatballs heaped in rice. It sounds innocuous, but frankly it looks like horse apples, or something excreted by a creature with an extremely agile digestive system.

All the Smart People Eat

If one were to come up with a parody of Depression-era food hints, it would be this: a book that posited toast as the epitome of clever, sophisticated dining. The food of the gods, no—but the food of Fred and Ginger? Perhaps.

By 1934, the nation's economy had reached its nadir; those who still had jobs feared tumbling into the black abyss of downward social mobility. Shuttered factories, soaped-up store windows, grizzled beggars, dust-bowl dirt-devils whirling on the newsreels, angry preachers screeching on the radio—Old Man Depression stalked the land with angry vengeance, and the nation seemed brittle and nervous. One might remember the good times 10 years before, when it seemed as if everyone would soon be rich . . . we'd all swim in champagne and take caviar mud baths before a night of croquet on the local Gatsby's lawn. But that all collapsed before most folks got the chance to enjoy the high life. How, then, might the average citizen be placated? How might one get a taste of the high life—in an affordable, Depression-era package?

Voilà: the Toastmaster. The humble bread toaster repositioned as a harbinger of sleek chic modernity. It was to the '30s what the fondue pot was to the recessionary '70s. Following are excerpts from this curious volume of pro-toast propaganda, written in a what-ho-old-thing trust-fund voice that must have comforted a great many socially nervous Americans. All the *right* people ate toast. All the *smart* people ate toast.

Here's

the cover of the book. You didn't just buy a Toastmaster—you bought the accessories, too. The segmented serving platter was divided into three zones: on the right, a dish that held the toast toppings; on the left, the bread staging area, where you kept the raw bread and used the oh-so-modern built-in slicer to whittle the toast into tiny rations; in the middle, the shining proof that someone was still willing to extend credit to your household: the toaster!

You can see the perils already—the slices are thin, the olives so big. Everything you made would fall in your lap. Perhaps this was a way to discourage guests from eating the olives and pickles. They'd just content themselves with toast. Fine: you could save the olives and pickles for later. For the drought. For the collapse. For the days when you huddled in the basement while the Bolsheviks roamed the countryside, shooting farmers and property owners . . .

But that's too horrible to contemplate. Here—have some toast and some things! Nothing says yum yum yum like a nice plate of *things*.

TOAST • AND • THINGS
A New American Art in Informal Entertainment

The

back cover of the book. Ladies, serve toast—and well-groomed twins in tuxedos will want to have sex with you!

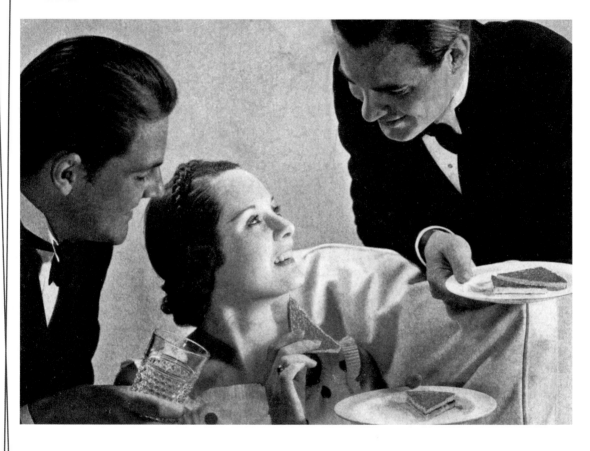

TOAST
FOR
HEALTH

APPETIZERS

(*or shall we say hors-d'oeuvres*)

The appetizer is not generally appreciated. Maybe that's because until Toast-and-Things became popular, they were apt to be de-appetizers. What is less appetizing than an appetizer that was put together, say, six hours before it is supposed to appetize? You've seen it yourself—how hungry men took two or three cocktails before they could summon courage to pick up something that looked—and tasted—like a cross between a fish, a bon-bon, and yesterday morning's toast.

TOASTMASTER has changed all that. Now appetizers are fresh and they're made right before your eyes. Crisp, hot toast *pops up,* you slide it under the cutting knife and divide it into good-manners size.

Then you put on the toast whatever pleases your taste. Caviar, anchovy, a bit of sausage—well, just look over the suggestions for arranging a TOASTMASTER HOSPITALITY TRAY that nobody can resist.

Toast-and-Things is certainly the answer to "What shall we serve with the cocktails?" And, you'll see how the interest and enthusiasm of making their own thaws out the most retiring, or important, guests.

To paraphrase: the Toastmaster takes away the alcoholic's most socially accepted pretext for gunning back three shots as soon as he joins the party.

"Gimme a rye, Bob. Thanks. Down the hatch!" (Gulp.) "Whew. Annnnd a refill, if you don't mind. Bottoms up!"

"Say, Phil, you want some anchovies?"

TOAST FOR HEALTH

"Whoa! Whoa Nellie, I'm not facing that undefinable appetizer while I'm sober. Another shot, if you don't mind there, pal . . . keep pouring . . . okay, well, if you say that's enough then I guess she'll do. Salut!" (Gulp.)

That's how it was in the good old days before that goddamn Toastmaster changed everything. Now Bob hands out ginger ale. A man has to have a slug in the car before the party if he wants to get a little glow going, and oh, how the little woman loves it when you do *that*. Then you head inside and see 'em all clustered around the toaster, sober as judges.

"Howza 'bouta little rye, Bob? Just a little drop for a thirsty fella?"

"No, Phil—we're using the interaction provided by public hors d'oeuvre assembly as a social lubricant! No more liquor. Say, what's the matter? You look a little nervous. C'mon—let's divide some crisped bread into good-manners sizes. It'll make a world of difference in your mood."

Phil walks unsteadily to the table, thinking: first Prohibition, now this. The nightmares just keep on coming.

CHILDREN'S PARTIES

Junior may be just big enough to hold a mug of milk in two hands, or he may have borrowed your razor this morning; and Sister—bless her heart—she may be in pig-tails or in Mother's best new stockings. What we mean is that their ages make no difference—load up a Toastmaster Hospitality Tray and you won't need to show them how to use it.

They take a lot for granted, these modern youngsters. Why, there are boys and girls in college today who never remember when there wasn't such a marvelous thing as Toastmaster! *{A college boy told us the other day that his earliest memory of his mother was as she sat at the wheel of her Cadillac and smoked a cigarette waiting for him to come out of kindergarten.}*

Boys and girls have changed somewhat since "when you and I were young, Maggie," but they still have appetites and friends. Lots of both. And they just naturally expect a proper parent to furnish a Toastmaster for their parties after school *{or at school!}* or on Saturdays, or after skating or swimming or dancing.

If this book came out in 1935, and the college boy was 20, then Mom was driving and publicly smoking in 1920. Mom was a flapper, and *you know what that means.* Hubba hubba, 23-skiddoo, I love my wife but oh you kid. Actually, the toast book is giving the middle-class sophisticate an opportunity for bemusement: it says that modern kids grew up in a world where Moms drove and smoked, and everyone had toasters. Why, in our day, children, Moms were beaten for driving and smoking, and only the Astors had a toaster.

Does this mean that kids understand how rare and special toast really is? No. But they're just kids. What else can you expect?

And why are you calling me Maggie?

TOAST
FOR
HEALTH

SUPPERS

The word "supper" doesn't always mean the same thing. For example, "supper" means something to the little girl—fourth from the end in the front row of the chorus—and then it means something else again to your Aunt Rachel from Dubuque.

But it makes no difference whether your mention of supper connotes champagne or iced tea, the Toastmaster Hospitality Tray will handle "supper" for you.

Because suppers may be so different, it's hard to set right down here in black and white precise recipes, or menus, for Toastmaster Hospitality Tray suppers. It depends on what kind of supper it is going to be, who are the guests, etc. So, what we suggest here is just by way of stimulating your imagination.

Let's say it's supper after theatre. It often is. Now, if you dined well on thick sirloin, or a spitted bird, you won't want exactly the kind of supper you'd like if—for example—you grabbed a malted milk and sandwich in order not to miss the opening scene of the play. Let's say you dined well. What can Toastmaster and Hospitality Tray suggest for supper?

Let's rerun this sentence, shall we, old thing? "Now, if you dined well on thick sirloin, or a spitted bird, you won't want exactly the kind of supper you'd like if—for example—you grabbed a malted milk and sandwich in order not to miss the opening scene of the play."

It makes sense . . . eventually. No doubt it made perfect sense to the ad writer, but he was light-headed and giddy from a diet of toast and beer.

Odd: buried away in the depths of a free pamphlet for a toaster, we learn the identity of the *New Yorker*'s fabled "little old lady from Dubuque." Her name was Aunt Rachel.

And here's another thought: would it have killed them to write sentences one could comprehend on the first pass? "The dishes with which both of the many Trays, being both the Hospitality Tray and the Breakfast tray, equipped thusly, as well as either of the Trays themselves, are without doubt of course usable together, or separately in any of the many ways of which a few or several or many will frequently occur to you." Good Lord! It's like the preamble to an 18th-century treatise on toast.

As for the Waters-Genter Company of Minneapolis, it no longer exists.

That's why you're not content. That's why the Western World has been stalked by ennui and existential dread since the early '50s, when Waters-Genter folded. You can't have one—and thus you are not content.

Explains everything, doesn't it?

TOAST FOR HEALTH

Bulletin No. 213

Old or young work or play

WE NEED Vitamins EVERY DAY

Even Fictional People Need Vitamins

Even poorly photographed people need vitamins. That's the message of this cheaply printed pamphlet. It seems to be an assemblage of every scrap of low-rent, royalty-free art the vitamin makers could find.

For instance: examine the sexually ambiguous couple at the top—why, it's Gertrude and Alice B., out for a spin. This bit of art was no doubt used a hundred times in the '50s and '60s for everything from geriatric blood supplements to . . . well, geriatric blood supplements.

Read on and meet our cast of characters. Just because they're stock doesn't mean they don't need vitamins.

$This$ is a family portrait. To be specific: this is a family portrait assembled by a muttering madman who lives in a basement apartment, eats bugs, watches the TV from a distance of one inch, and constructs imaginary families by cutting pictures from magazines and adhering them to the wall with a paste made of ear wax and phlegm.

Mom on the left suffers from low-contrast blood, and often just . . . fades away into an indistinct blur, sometimes taking one-tooth junior with her. Behind her stands walleyed Grandma; pity the fool who falls under the gaze of that dead gray right eye. Then there's Little Master Boomer Baby, 14 years away from being stamped A-1 'Nam fodder; he may or may not be sitting on the knee of Standard Dad, a fine upstanding fellow who works at Consolidated Inventory, where he's employed as an inventory consolidator. This picture was taken after he'd had his second old-fashioned. That's surely his daughter leaning against his arm, but who is that grinning apparition behind him? It's Satan's insurance agent! He's given them all coverage—with *Mutual of Beelzebub!*

ALL YOUR LIFE
and all your family

From the time you are a baby, all through your life, Vitamins and Minerals help you.

Yes, as we grow older, we tire of our partners and practice strangling them now and then. Appetite may grow "more changeable," as the pamphlet puts it. Older people need to eat less, but still need their vitamins.

But why? As this picture clearly indicates, old people don't need food at all, because they soon turn into marble busts commissioned by a Bulgarian commissar of culture.

As we grow older - -

If you're not sick but feel all worn-out - -

because you are not getting enough vitamins, try Liver, Iron, B-1, B-2, B-12 or Multi-Vitamin-Minerals. Many minor ailments and "don't-feel-very-good" cases can be traced to lack of proper vitamins and minerals.

Odd how this never came up in any of the classic noir movies or novels. When a dame walked into a detective's office, leveled that dead dry gaze at his skeptical face, announced she'd had it with the bum and she wanted the proof to get her a ticket to Splitsburg—well, the detective took her at her word. The detective thought: She's had a bad patch. She's been done wrong. That's why she looks so low.

The detective never said: "Maybe you should eat some liver."

Although that might have made for snappy repartee: "Maybe you should eat some yourself, Shamus." But then the detective brings out the pamphlet and tries to sell her supplements . . . no, it would have ruined the entire genre. Although we all know Marlowe sold Amway on the side. Hey: it paid the rent.

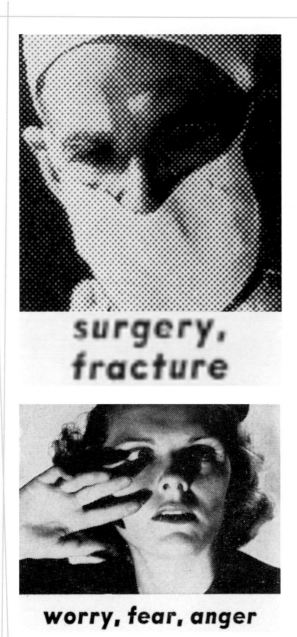

surgery,
fracture

worry, fear, anger

Who needs vitamins? Brother, who doesn't? This is a partial list of situations that require extra vitamin intake.

Here's what you want to see right before the gas kicks in.

And doing the Batusi. Or rather: not paying attention while doing the Batusi. Remember, friends:

Eating itself is a form of stress.

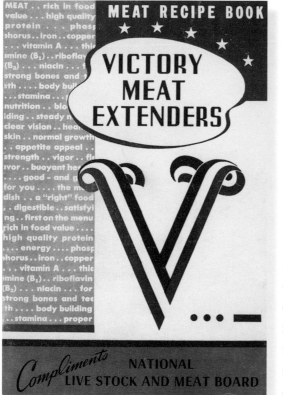

MEAT RECIPE BOOK

VICTORY MEAT EXTENDERS

MEAT . . rich in food value . . . high quality protein . . . phosphorus . . iron . . copper . . . vitamin A . . . thiamine (B₁) . . riboflavin (B₂) . . . niacin . . . strong bones and teeth . . . . body building . . . stamina . . . nutrition . . blood building . . steady nerves clear vision . . healthy skin . . normal growth . . appetite appeal . . strength . . vigor . . flavor . . buoyant health . . . . good – and good for you . . . the main dish . . a "right" food . . digestible . . satisfying . . first on the menu rich in food value . . . . high quality protein . . . energy . . phosphorus . . iron . . copper . . . vitamin A . . . thiamine (B₁) . . riboflavin (B₂) . . . niacin . . . for strong bones and teeth . . . . body building . . . stamina . . . proper

Compliments NATIONAL LIVE STOCK AND MEAT BOARD

Eat Brains and Whip Hitler!

In retrospect, it might have been better to increase civilian meat production. Abandon gas rationing. Forget the scrap drives, the exhortations to can every vegetable, husband every jot of fat that drips from the precious roast. These are grim reminders that the war is going badly. In retrospect, perhaps the government should have sealed off five or six Midwestern states, left the locals to starve, and bumped up rations for everyone else. Cruel? Yes. But think of Johnny, getting a letter from home while he squats in a foxhole. He wants to read of juicy steaks, turkey dinners, the meaty bounty of the America for which he fights. And he learns that Mom and Dad are reduced to eating . . .

VICTORY MENU
SUPPER
Topsy Turvy Meat Pie
Shoestring Potatoes
Carrot Strips - Celery
Jellied Fruit Salad
Chocolate Cake
Coffee

CREAMED BRAINS ON TOAST

Or, worst of all, Private Johnny learns that his folks are eating . . . ZOMBIE FOOD.

To modern ears, this sounds like a Zappa album: Creamed Brains on Toast. Or a public service announcement telling kids not to use drugs. *This is your brain. These are your brains, creamed. These are your brains, creamed, on toast.*

In fact, these were your brains, and this was your supper. But don't worry that the nation's supply of brains might run out—we've many more dishes to thrill your jaded palate:

LIVER SPOON CAKES

BRAISED HEART WITH STUFFING

It's the braising that makes the dish. And what might it be stuffed with, eh? Perhaps—*brains?*

TONGUE ROLLS FLORENTINE

TONGUE WITH CARROTS IN SPINACH NESTS
4 pounds tongue — Serves 12

If there's a definition of good times, it's this: "Not a lot of tongue-based meals." Oh, they try to dress it up, drizzle foreign names over it, give it cute birdy forms, but it doesn't disguise the basic tongueness of the dish. Tongue is what you eat when you're out of marrow stew and Ring O' Rectum Flan.

On a related note: when serving other filtration and extraction organs, block them into shapes that do not recall their original contours.

KIDNEY LOAF

The Pledge of the American Homemaker

I pledge the nation that my mission
Will be to practice good nutrition;
To plan those meals which every day
Yield energy for work and play;
Meals which supply the strength that wins,
With protein — minerals — vitamins.

I pledge my service to the nation
To do my part in conservation.
The rules of cooking I'll observe.
Each bit of food I will conserve.
With all the problems to be faced,
I'll do my best to outlaw waste.

I want to do my bit and more,
To help America win the war.

— H. Howard Biggar

No one can argue with the sentiments, but one has to ask: did any American Homemaker actually take this pledge? Perhaps the local newspaper—in the women's section, of course—announced that a certain handsome movie star, recently drafted to fight for the War Department's new Morale Division, would be coming to town Saturday afternoon, and all ladies from the Kitchen Corps were hereby ordered to fall in. So they dutifully went to the Bijou, where some broad-shouldered extra with an Ipana smile led them in the pledge.

And remember, gals—Hitler loves it when you squander suet!

Perhaps. But this was America. The pledge was not legally binding.

MEAT · CENTER OF VICTORY MEALS

Ham Shanks and Cabbage

Chock-

Full

of

Vitamins

and

Minerals

Put another way: Pig Ass with the Bones Still in It. Or, perhaps, Oinker Cheeks. However you describe the dish, it's clear that the war was a much closer affair than we recognize today. Modern Americans would rather surrender—to anyone!—than eat something like this.

Meat might indeed have been the center of victory meals, but that seems a rather cruel thing to point out when this is how meat gets defined. It's like saying: Marrow & Suet Frosting—Center of Victory Desserts.

MEAT • CENTER OF VICTORY MEALS

Call VEGETABLES INTO SERVICE

THEY MUST PASS INSPECTION

Select fresh, crisp vegetables free from blemishes, decay and soft spots. Bruised and wilted vegetables have lost their vitamins.

WHEN THEY ARE INDUCTED

Clean and wash, remove spoiled spots from perishable vegetables and store in refrigerator until ready for use.

Keep crisp pod or leafy vegetables in crisper or wet cloth bag. Use these vegetables as soon after buying as possible as they gradually lose vitamins on standing.

Keep vegetables like onions and potatoes in a dry, cool place.

PREPARE FOR COMBAT

Wash vegetables thoroughly but quickly. They lose food value if soaked in water.

Have skin on vegetables when possible. Pare thinly, if at all. Minerals and vitamins lie close to the skin.

If cutting vegetables small, chop, shred or cut just before cooking or preparing salad to retain the most minerals and vitamins.

PREVENT MASS EXECUTION *of Vitamins* ... AND KILLING *of Flavor*

SUBMARINE ATTACKS Sink *the Minerals and Vitamins*
Cook in smallest possible amount of water.

AIR RAIDS *Fatal to Vitamin C*
Cook tightly covered to avoid exposure to air. Don't stir in air.

CONTINUOUS FIRE *Destroys Vitamins*
Have water boiling, salted. Bring vegetables to boil quickly. Turn down heat and simmer—just until tender (to keep crisp texture).

GENERAL STRATEGY

To retain color, texture and food value, prepare *just before time to cook—cook just till tender—serve as soon as cooked.* Save liquid left after vegetables are cooked. It contains minerals and vitamins dissolved out of the vegetables. Use in soups, gravies, etc.

16 ... Vegetables

COMMANDO TACTICS

Exceptions to general rule—see page 19. Plunge frozen vegetables into rapidly boiling water and cook just till tender (vitamin and mineral value about same as in fresh). Heat *canned vegetables* in own liquor (boiled down one-half) 20 min. for non-acid vegetables.

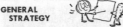

Vitamins

had a role on the home front, too. This is a page from a book of Betty Crocker's wartime hints. "Call vegetables into service"—okay, fine. Inspection, induction—cute.

But *"Prevent Mass Execution of Vitamins . . . and the KILLING of Flavor"*? With submarine attacks, air raids, and continuous fire?

Is this really what women wanted to read while standing at the kitchen sink, waiting for a letter?

restaurant-tested . . . for your home

SPECIALTIES OF THE HOUSE

macaroni • spaghetti • noodles

COOK BOOK of Durum Wheat Main Dishes

. . . a selection of outstanding recipes from well-known eating places, adapted for home use.

Specialties of the House

This is where it began, right here. In 1996 I went home to Fargo and found an ancient recipe book in my mom's cupboard: *Specialties of the House,* from the North Dakota State Durum Wheat Commission. It was full of ghastly pictures, and I did a column on it for the *Pioneer Press,* where I was then employed. Later, when I was starting to play with the Internet, I decided to make a website out of the booklet. I'd purchased some old *Life* magazines for clip art, and I decided to toss in some old food ads. Voilà: the original Gallery of Regrettable Food.

It had its 15 minutes of fame: Cool Site of the Week here and there, a brief mention on CNN. This led to print mentions all over the place. A flurry of e-mail from New Zealanders told me they'd read about it in their local papers; ditto some mail from England, where it was featured in the *Guardian.* The BBC did a small story on it. Then Australian radio. Then Canadian radio. That was years ago, and it never ends. As I was working on this very page to prepare the Gallery for its book incarnation, I took a break to make lunch and picked up the Sunday paper. It had a small story about the Gallery.

Specialties of the House is the heart and soul of the Gallery, the Dead Sea text. If the Welcome Wagon hadn't dropped off this book when my parents moved to North Fargo in 1962, there would have been no Gallery 34 years later.

Note: This wouldn't have been a good thing. Really.

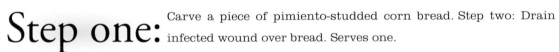

Step one:
Carve a piece of pimiento-studded corn bread. Step two: Drain infected wound over bread. Serves one.

This plate, incidentally, is identical to the ones used by the Elim Lutheran Church in Fargo, North Dakota. I don't know why I remember that, but I do.

A nice warm bowl of albino intestines, heart parts, and ALPO? Why, *yes*, please!

Nothing

quite says "burnt, cold cheese" like a picture of burnt, cold cheese. For a festive touch, garnish the dish with a starfish beaten to a bloody pulp.

Add parsley for no particular reason other than that's the way we've done things for 50 years 'round these parts, and who are you to come along and say we should do otherwise, mister? All right, then.

Rice

Krispie Bar with Ketchup! Mmm! Not really. It's a Macaroni Meat Loaf Bar, à la the Sputumbric. A bar of beige beef with a gout of lurid ketchup and charred asparagus. Dig in!

The caption informs us that this dish is recommended by Winnifred Pendigrast, nutritionist for the Detroit school system.

Note: Detroit's population has been reduced by two-thirds since this photo was taken.

Coincidence. Sheer . . . coincidence.

Roadkill?

No, no. This is Ironed Chicken with Tomato Fragments.

For a curiously Masonic touch, there's a disembodied eye floating in the middle of the dish, just like that one on the back of a dollar bill. For that matter, this meal appears to be giving *itself* the secret Masonic handshake.

Remember: This photo is supposed to make you hungry. It's supposed to make you *want* to eat this dish. I last saw this in a *Star Trek* episode; it stuck on Spock's back and made him go insane.

J**ust** as a test, I showed this to my pregnant wife; she's been having some . . . food issues lately. This was only a test.

That was two days ago. I'm still not forgiven. Nor should I be.

Something

-or-Other with Cream Sauce and Mushrooms. Unfortunately, it looks like something you'd see after eating bad mushrooms, not before. I do like the way the other dishes have surrounded it in a threatening fashion, as if they intend to shove it off the table for the benefit of all.

And so ends *Specialties of the House.* Thanks to the North Dakota State Durum Wheat Commission for all the fun, and, yes, we'll all continue to enjoy spaghetti.

Despite your best efforts to persuade us otherwise.

About the Author

James Lileks is a syndicated columnist for Newhouse News Service. His popular website, "The Official Institute of Good Cheer," on which *The Gallery of Regrettable Food* is based, can be seen at www.lileks.com

If you enjoyed this book, you might find yourself temporarily bemused by its cumbersome, amateurish online version. Bereft of the professional's touch, rife with errors, impenetrably constructed, www.lileks.com awaits your visits.* If you enjoyed paying for this book, please do not visit this site; www.lileks.com is the incubator for future projects, and as such is provided free of charge.

To repeat: Hours of free enjoyment are yours at www.lileks.com. If you find yourself paying for them in book form in the future, you've only yourself to blame.

*Computer required to access the Internet.